I0104958

Quarterly Essay

CONTENTS

Quarterly Essay is published four times a year by Black Inc., an imprint of Schwartz Publishing Pty Ltd. Publisher: Morry Schwartz.

ISBN 9781863952156 ISSN 1832-0953

Subscriptions – 1 year (4 issues): $49 within Australia incl. GST. Outside Australia $79.
2 years (8 issues): $95 within Australia incl. GST. Outside Australia $155.
Payment may be made by Mastercard, Visa or Bankcard, or by cheque made out to Schwartz Publishing. Payment includes postage and handling.

To subscribe, fill out and post the subscription card, or subscribe online at:

www.quarterlyessay.com

Correspondence and subscriptions should be addressed to the Editor at:

Black Inc. Level 5, 289 Flinders Lane Melbourne VIC 3000 Australia
Phone: 61 3 9654 2000 / Fax: 61 3 9654 2290
Email:
quarterlyessay@blackincbooks.com (editorial)
subscribe@blackincbooks.com (subscriptions)

Editor: Chris Feik / Management: Sophy Williams
Publicity: Anna Lensky / Design: Guy Mirabella
Production Co-ordinator: Caitlin Yates

NOTE ON STYLE

If there is an us-and-themness to this story, which rudely assumes the reader is non-Aboriginal, I apologise, but as a white man I cannot do other than stand on the outside and look in. Nor do I seek to sign up to the growing white Australian sport of claiming a Warlpiri, Pintupi, Pitjantjatjara or Noongar great-grandmother in my heritage. None exists.

Besides, Aborigines are used to being talked about rather than talked to, are they not? Perhaps this is something I picked up from the previous PM, who always seemed so disconnected from and baffled by Aborigines. He could only talk of "them," whereas he found it easier to gather up the great white suburban clans close to his breast and talk of "us."

I also try to avoid using the term "full-blood" and refer to the Aborigines who are the direct target of the federal government's emergency intervention as "bush" or "tribal" or "remote-area" or "town-camp" Aborigines. The term full-blood, regarded by some as pejorative, is still in wide circulation, particularly among full-blood Aborigines themselves. Part-Aborigines take umbrage at it, and indeed at the term part-Aboriginal. They believe no distinction should be drawn between degrees of Aboriginality. It is one of the wounds of the stolen generations, of being the in-between people, not quite accepted by full-bloods or full-whites. And if such people have grown up with whites calling them coons or boongs or niggers or blacks, I understand why they would wish to identify as straight Aboriginal ahead of the non-Aboriginal parts of their make-up.

Around the nation, as well, there has been a creep back to our grandparents' style of using "Aboriginal" as a noun. The *West Australian* newspaper, I've noticed, has taken to talking of "an Aboriginal" or "a group of Aboriginals." I prefer "Aboriginal" used as an adjective.

A final point: I have been told that I ought not use the term "Aborigine" or "Aborigines" in a freestanding way: out of politeness, I should instead refer to an "Aboriginal *person*" or to "Aboriginal *people*." I don't agree. An Aborigine is, by any reasonable modern definition, a person.

Paul Toohey

LAST DRINKS

The Impact of the Northern
Territory Intervention

Paul Toohey

If I got one thing against the black chappies, it's this: no one gives it to you; you got to take it. —Francis Costello, New York-Irish gangster in *The Departed*

Give me a thousand acres of tractable land & all the gang members that exist & you'll see the Authentic alternative lifestyle, the Agrarian one. —Bob Dylan, liner notes to *World Gone Wrong*

TOM ROBINSON, AND FRIENDS

All of us wanted our parents to be gentle. Some of us got it, some didn't. Mostly we needed our parents to protect us. A home may have had an open gate and an unlocked front door, but it needed to be a sanctuary, watched over by protective eyes, a place where children were permitted to grow without being subject to interference from groping hands. But what if the greatest threat to a home came not from outside its walls, but from within? Such was the charge levelled against Aborigines on 21 June 2007, the day the intervention was announced: of forming a parental Fifth Column that molested and raped children while ignoring their more mundane rights to be fed, washed and educated.

The initial effect of the emergency federal intervention in the Northern Territory on the grounds of child sex abuse was to accuse remote-area Aborigines en masse of failing to provide their children with these fundamental protections and human rights. These were no less than charges of crimes against humanity – their own humanity. It is hard to find another example, recent or past, of one race being so singled out for failing to nurture its children, or charged with turning so inwardly against its most intimate relations. Even in nature, animals have their reasons for abandoning or devouring their young. Being stuck on the piss, or stuck on the gambling blanket, is no reason.

We were asked to accept that Aborigines, after 60,000 years of survival in some of the most hellishly harsh country known to humans, had, in the last forty years, forgotten how to raise children: that the part of the Aboriginal DNA allotted to parenthood had been cast adrift from the genome or, perhaps, was never really there. While the emergency intervention sought a better future, its thinking took us into the past, straight back to a time when the Land Rover, not the Land Cruiser, was the preferred vehicle of the north, and when conventional wisdom among white Australians was that Aborigines had inbuilt character flaws and a generally weak genetic disposition that marked them for extinction.

When Sir Les Patterson called Aborigines a "great little bunch of blokes," those of us who had white Australian grandparents or great-grandparents may have heard their words rising from the grave. They talked in similar terms, fondly, but always with a cancelling clause: "Your Aborigine is by and large a decent fellow who cannot handle his drink"; or, "The Aborigine cannot work because he feels too strongly the lure of his ancestors. He prefers to go walkabout than work."

Late last year, passing through Katherine, I heard an older white woman describing a powerfully built young Aboriginal man as a "strapping

Warlpiri buck." I sensed a hint of Mandingo longing in her voice, and while the rutting-savage suggestiveness of the term transported me directly to the deep south, it was not to a sexually pent-up slave plantation but rather a scene in *To Kill a Mockingbird*: Tom Robinson is sitting in the dock, accused of rape and unequipped to answer to the white folks who'd already made up their minds.

The ease with which bush Aborigines were assumed to be either sexual predators who would, as a matter of course and convenience, rape children (fathers and uncles), or accomplices who'd turn a blind eye (mothers and aunts), was depressing and dehumanising. As the failed Aboriginal welfare system was revamped through the part-quarantining of hand-out money in order to awaken indigenous people from the long sleep, to get them to school and to work, the intervention, or emergency response, looked like yet another form of welfare state, fashioned to once again wipe the arses of Australia's first people.

It would have been nice if, by 2008, we'd moved on. Instead, time had stood still for three decades in the bush. It started with the mid-'70s granting of land rights, powerful law by which white Australia sought to make amends and recognise that traditional Aborigines had ceremonial responsibilities and a connection to country that went well beyond any white notion of real estate. Land rights was the national Berocca, designed to fix us up after a long night on the blacks, and after that to … what, exactly? To give Aborigines what was rightly theirs while at the same time condemning them to the expectation – ours, not theirs – that they should revert to hunter-gatherer basics? We admired the resourcefulness and dexterity of Aboriginal hunters but sneered when we saw a Toyota and a gun being employed in the kill. Adapting was never going to be easy – for us, that is, not them. They, on the other hand, learned to run us ragged.

In post-land-rights times, Aborigines refined their ancient capacity for sitting, watching, opportunistically waiting for game to pass their way. They did this by wrapping outsiders around their fingers. They were shockingly effective at not managing their affairs and delegating responsibility elsewhere. They would sit back and watch the new white manager do his head in as he tried to come to grips with Aboriginal time – meaning, "maybe tomorrow, most probably the day after." These managers would eventually succumb to Aboriginal demands which, on a strict interpretation, involved corruption. Common examples: a senior person wanted to use the council's four-wheel-drive to go to town for a break, or to visit their outstation, using the community's diesel; or asked the CDEP wages manager to overlook his non-attendance and pay him for un-worked hours. Aborigines saw this as good sport, as well as being vital to them maintaining mobility and income. But they rarely considered, until it was too late, that by demanding favours they, in turn, ceded power to these white managers, who quickly learned to use their detailed knowledge of everyone's personal business to wrest complete control of communities. Fiefdoms were born.

In 2006, in the large western Arnhem Land town of Maningrida, the joint was, as always, ankle-deep in rubbish. It wasn't such a bad place overall, yet at that time the new Families, Community Services and Indigenous Affairs Minister, Mal Brough, and his senior departmental cronies were flying about the north looking for trouble. I put it to a white manager: "Why don't you clean the place up? You know this mess is the first thing the politicians and bureaucrats will see. Why not show them the place is superficially functional as well as at a deeper level? Pay people to clean the place up – if not for the politicians, just because it's the hygienic thing to do. It'll take you two days." I was told: "Aborigines do not understand rubbish. They come from a society where everything – skins, bones, fur – would break down. Rubbish is not cultural." What magnificent bullshit.

If the people of Maningrida did not have the mind-power to realise that plastic tended not to break down, why then were they trying to address illegal fishing incursions by Indonesian sharking vessels into their waters? They were doing this for four good reasons: they took offence that outsiders would plunder their coastline without permission; they were well aware that quarantine breaches, such as the entry of rabid monkeys, could do great damage to their country; they wanted to be recognised as accredited sea rangers with the power to repel or even detain invaders; and discarded plastic long lines and gill nets were floating around the local seas, creating invisible walls of death that were strangling turtles and everything else caught up in them. Modern rubbish was affecting traditional hunting.

Aborigines were accomplished at seeing things selectively. But did rubbish have anything to do with the intervention that was soon to come? It did, but only because Brough was looking for any excuse to force his will on the bush. Why give him one? The people of Maningrida would soon be confronted with a hideous gang-rape sex case. One that, just like the rubbish, appeared to involve many people turning their backs on what they had seen.

It hadn't helped anyone that the considerable commercial potential of land rights had not been realised. "Land rich and dirt poor" was the truism, but it remained a fitting enough description of what land rights had delivered. The philosophy of land rights was all about acknowledgment, reparation and preservation of culture: there was never any demand that Aboriginal enterprises spring to life on Aboriginal land ... but there was an expectation that some would get going. You'd fly into Cairns airport in the east, or Broome to the west, and be hit with all sorts of baggage-carousel offers to give you a genuine Aboriginal experience. Some appeared kitsch, some boring. If the idea of stalking through the outback looking for bush tucker – bits of plant given reassuring Western names to assist in their digestion, such as "bush tomato" or "bush banana" – was your thing, you could go for it. At least there was the opportunity to meet Aborigines. Fly into Darwin, though, and you, German tourist, arriving in Australia's Aboriginal heartland, were offered precisely nothing. If Territory Aborigines did not want to expose themselves to visitors or scrutiny, or see themselves as storefront Indians, well, fair enough – but don't bother claiming to be misunderstood.

Very few Northern Territory Aborigines ran the kinds of business that might pull them off welfare and see them become, even modestly, independently wealthy. Every enterprise that did exist seemed connected to a government-backed scheme, or involved white businesses – usually cattle, mining, fishing or wilderness tourism – paying for use of Aboriginal land but not using Aboriginal workers. The outsiders were always saying they wanted to use Aboriginal workers, so where were they? "You are not to quote me on this, and I mean it," said a Territory government staffer who was trying to understand the impasse. "The reason's simple: they're lazy." There was no point beating around the bush – he was right. Or, to see it their way, there was a point beating around the bush in a clapped-out 80-Series Toyota wagon full of kids, gunning down magpie geese, braining fat file snakes in creek crossings and catching big lazy fish in scum-stilled waterholes with homemade lures.

And I'd admit to my envy. Thanks to land rights, Aborigines had been afforded a luxury known to very few non-indigenous mortgage holders: they could sleep without ever worrying that someone was going to reef what was theirs from beneath them. No bank could ever foreclose on Aboriginal land, because it could not be sold or traded. Many family groups had outstation houses – powered by beautiful government-gifted solar systems – along with houses in town. They didn't have to buy these residences or pay for repairs when they were trashed. What kept them awake at night was the ghetto-blaster blaring from the home of the local grog runner, who'd managed to successfully infiltrate back into his community with a stockpile of 750ml Jim Beam bottles and warm VB. That, and the gangs of kids trying to steal the community ambulance.

Lazy? A generalisation, for sure – but not quite as bad as saying all your men were child molesters. Several years ago, when I was visiting a Western Australian community, a young mother turned up at the clinic with a very sick young child whose breathing was too shallow. The flying doctor was arriving from Alice around midnight. The whole town knew the plane was coming; everyone let it be known they were deeply concerned.

At about 11 p.m., the town's white manager, Mike Harper, and I went out to the dirt airstrip. Harper removed the padlock from a shipping container and brought out big boxes of battery-powered torches, those little lamps which sit up on their tails, and we began marching up either side of the strip, setting them up as the landing lights for the plane. I said to Harper: "Why aren't any local people helping?" I'll leave Harper's reply where it ended up − scattered into a million bits in the Western Desert wind. A magnificent, brand-new, single-propeller medical plane (this was no Cessna; it was huge, Swiss-made, apparently) touched down. The white nurse delivered mother and baby to the plane's steps. It took off and we walked back up the strip, collecting hundreds of lamps and returning them to the shipping container. The process took hours. Not one community resident had turned up to help, or to see off the precious cargo.

Late last year I came upon a ratty van stopped axle-deep in an Arnhem Land creek, near a populated outstation. There was an adult man and five grown teenage boys sitting around a tiny fire in the creek-side sand. The man asked for a push-start − that is, he wanted me to push his car by putting my bull-bar against his back bumper. I asked him: "How long have you been sitting here?" He shrugged: "Long time." I said: "Did you try to push-start it yourselves?" Blank look. I asked: "Why didn't you just get these boys to push-start it?" He shrugged again. I asked the boys the same question and got a combination of cold stares and sheepish looks. I would have driven on and left them to their remarkable apathy had the van not been blocking my path. Upon my bullbar meeting their bumper, I pushed the car a mere metre before it coughed to life.

Confronted with such wilful futility you might be inclined to wonder if there was a cultural reason for them not pushing the van. And when I say "you might," I mean it − because I wasn't. However, overtaking the van, and making sure they wore more of my dust than needed, I tried to clear my brain of exasperation and imagine a time long ago, in the days before WD-40, when this road was rarely travelled and anyone with a wet distributor cap had to unclip it, blow it dry and, if that didn't work, push the fucking car. These thoughts failed me. They were too rational, too obvious. In my irritation I wondered: would the nearest foreign neighbours of these people, the Timorese, ever take such a slothful approach to an engine's wet electricals? No. They'd heave-to.

A bit further along the track, as my infuriation subsided, I thought: these people are just not in any hurry. I guessed that's what happened when you didn't have a job, but nor did you see yourself as unemployed. You had a life. Sort of. Like I wish I did. Sort of.

These people had become accustomed to doing nothing for themselves.

Land rights brought isolation, deprivation and indolence, but it also permitted traditional culture to flourish. Some time back, while on a work trip to Ngukurr in the lower reaches of Arnhem Land, a friend and I took a wrong turn down a dirt track. We were looking for someone. We came upon a startling site – maybe 100 people, seated three-deep in a circle. There were people dancing in the middle and a man was prowling about, talking up the crowd in the manner of an evangelist. We noticed men with great ochre circles, outlined in white, on their chests. There were women and children present, meaning it wasn't secret business. And there was no sign of any white film crew.

I backed the Toyota up fast, with apologetic waves which were accepted with goodwill. I felt that faint wrench of envy – not because I would ever wish to be indoctrinated by a tribe, nor because I desired to know their ceremonial business, but because of the sense of occasion and unity and, most of all, kinship, that I had so fleetingly witnessed. I came from a big family, so that part of it was covered: but I had never got the extended sense of it – never at a football game, never at a concert … though maybe once at a black church in Memphis on a Sunday morning. This ceremony was more intimate, and on a scale with which I was not familiar. Outsiders often called it "culture," but there were better words for it: community, or family.

Family also meant forgiveness. For just about anything. In June 2004, a 54-year-old man, GJ, took his promised fourteen-year-old child bride, smashed her about with boomerangs and then dragged her off to his outstation where he had, according to the charge sheet, non-consensual anal intercourse. The anal aspect was curious though never explained in court or elsewhere. Maybe he didn't want her getting pregnant; maybe he was a sexual extremist. The girl had returned to her community on school holidays and that was what she got. It was an outrage that GJ was never charged with rape.

The girl's grandmother was on GJ's side: she believed the girl was hanging out with a boyfriend, possibly having sex with him instead of saving herself for old GJ. The girl had been betrothed to GJ from birth; she was his promised bride and the girl's family had taken payments in various ways from GJ through the years. The grandmother participated in the bashing of her granddaughter. GJ got a month from the Territory's new chief justice, Brian Martin, though this was later overturned and a longer sentence imposed.

There was also the earlier case of Maningrida's Jackie Pascoe, who as a 49-year-old in 2001 did a near-identical thing to his fifteen-year-old child bride. The girl's family had consented to Pascoe taking the girl to his outstation. They'd for years been taking down-payments from Pascoe for her betrothal, in the form of spears, food and cash. It was a traditional arrangement.

At the magistrate's hearing, prosecution and defence had by then agreed to put to the court a drastically toned-down version of what really happened. At Pascoe's outstation, the court heard, Pascoe "told the victim to take off her clothes and the victim complied. The defendant then got on top of the victim. The defendant removed his shorts and had penile vaginal intercourse with the victim." It was, according to the lawyers, consensual. On the following day, some friends of the girl came to collect her because she wanted to go back home to Maningrida. Pascoe got angry and repelled the friends by firing an unlicensed and unregistered shotgun in the air.

It was dressed up as an arranged customary "marriage" which had gone slightly awry.

Pascoe was initially charged with rape, though the terrified girl, who realised she would have to confront a member of a powerful Arnhem Land family in court, withdrew the charges. A carnal-knowledge charge was the best the cops could come up with. Pascoe pleaded guilty to having sexual intercourse with a female under the age of sixteen years and to illegal firearm discharge and possession. A magistrate gave him four months and fined him for the shotgun.

The prosecution and the defence could not be blamed for the fact that the girl had withdrawn charges. And at least Pascoe was charged with something. However, this short sentence was too much for Pascoe's lawyers, who immediately won bail and announced they would appeal – even though they knew the nature of the girl's original complaint. They wanted to turn it into a case of a hard-done-by customary-law husband.

I had obtained the girl's original police statement, which revealed she was anything but a compliant child bride. "I was listening to that tape on that stereo – the music was Backstreet Boys," she told police. "He told me to shut the door, I said leave it open. He forced me to shut that door, he made me frightened. He started slapping my face and then punching me. He used his right and left hand to slap me in my face, he was hitting me real hard. He had that closed fist and he hit me eight times. I was feeling dizzy and he said: 'Let me look, so I can hit you again.'

"I said to him I want to go out and have a drink of water and wash my face. He said: 'No, you're not going anywhere, no phone call, no truck [out] for you.' He told me to take off my clothes, so I did. He grabbed me by my left arm and my right leg and threw me onto that mattress. He put his foot onto my neck and he was pushing me down on that mattress. He had my right arm and he was twisting it – it felt like he would break it ... the blood came from my nose. He was on top of me and he forced me, and I was laying down and trying to cross my legs." The next day the girl tried to leave Pascoe's outstation with her friends, but Pascoe fired the unregistered shotgun in the air and kept her back.

The Supreme Court appellant judge, John Gallop, saw no issue – he said the girl "knew what was expected of her" in customary law. Pascoe had already served a short manslaughter term for skinning alive a previous girlfriend, though neither prosecution nor the defence seemed in any hurry to mention this to the judge. Pascoe, with the full consent of the prosecution, was dealt with as a minor offender. He was sentenced to 24 hours' prison for the sexual assault, and 14 days for the firearm. There was, of course, an outcry. The Territory Aboriginal parliamentarian John

Ah Kit said the judge had "failed in his broader duty to the law of the Northern Territory, the nation and the international community." The embarrassed Office of the Director of Public Prosecutions reassessed its position and appealed. Pascoe was re-sentenced to twelve months, suspended after one month.

The white court system permitted grotesque distortions of the facts, and the black law of western Arnhem Land was no better. It didn't seek to protect the victim – it was only interested in which of the adversaries was the more powerful. Inevitably, it was not the complainant. Weak tribal position might explain why they were victimised in the first place.

Important lawyers wrote articles about Pascoe's rights. Darwin-based Rex Wild, QC, was the Director of Public Prosecutions when both the GJ and Pascoe cases were alive: he was aware of the cases and it was his lawyers who were in the Supreme Court, agreeing with the defence that the men should receive bare-minimum sentences, only to turn around and appeal when the depth of public disquiet became known. Rex Wild would later be appointed to co-head the *Little Children Are Sacred* inquiry.

GJ's and Pascoe's cases were important cases that deserved the strong national debate they received. But missing from the discussion were voices from the ground in the north. By the time the intervention arrived, the bush was unprepared to meet the allegation that Aboriginal men were by and large child-rapists, or that women in their silence were co-conspirators. There was no one to speak for the bush. Since the departure of Galarrwuy Yunupingu from the chairmanship of the Northern Land Council, and the death of Gatjil Djerrkura, the inaugural chairman of ATSIC, there had been no stand-out Aboriginal leader operating in the Territory, whether man or woman, firebrand or considerate, urban- or bush-based, from within politics or from its outskirts. The director of the Central Land Council, David Ross, was always a strong spokesman, but lacked traditional authority and didn't carry the imprimatur of some of the Aboriginal leaders who'd gone before. The leadership void in the far north of the Territory, where most Aborigines lived, was stark; no one had put up their hand. No erudite Noel Pearson-type. Yunupingu was a compelling tribal leader, who could and would pull rank on urban blacks and federal politicians alike, because he really was a man who lived in the bush (albeit in a fine house), and really did have complex ceremonial responsibilities, not just some half-lost concept of what his or her Dreaming might be. But his messages were at times mixed and he appeared not to speak for Aborigines at large but primarily for himself. There were several capable Aboriginal Labor parliamentarians, but they were constrained by their party and rarely permitted to air their true thoughts.

The intervention did something remarkable. All that fighting talk we were so used to from politicised Aborigines, of "200 years of white invasion" and its ugly offspring, "genocide," had been ripped from Aboriginal mouths and thrown right back in their faces. Now it was they who stood accused of slow-burn genocide, of conducting a systemic sexual invasion against their own young.

But was it a fair cop? Would you, as a remote-area Aboriginal parent who had managed to raise and house and feed children despite the great obstacles – the most basic of which might be having no access to a fridge and washing machine – have had a right to feel just a little wounded, a little angry, that you had been branded as the most failed kind of human being on the planet? Might you not wonder how it all came to this? All those missionaries and teachers and cops and nurses and government-types and land-council staffers and anthropologists, all of them in their acronym-doored white Troop Carriers, bush hats and sturdy shoes, who over the years had come to your secluded communities to ridicule the notion of self-determination, and who would secretly drink their red wine and cold beer and smoke joints behind locked cyclone fences as the sun set on another hard day's pointless hand-wringing in paradise-hell ... didn't they have some explaining to do? Perhaps, but such people were the mere tiny creatures of policy. Policy itself wore no recognisable face in the bush, unless it was miserable underspending. It was rarely ever called upon to explain itself except at election time.

Yet it was not in the bush that Aborigines were most suffering or harming each other. When a murder occurred in Yirrkala or Lajamanu or Maningrida, you had to search back years to find the previous killing. There were too many suicides, everywhere, and there had been sexual-assault cases like GJ's and Pascoe's – but the fact that GJ's and Pascoe's victims had initially gathered the nerve to complain to police suggested a real attitude shift in the bush; these courageous teenagers were no longer prepared to be sexually ransacked for the sake of ancient lore. They wanted boyfriends their own age. What let these girls down, more than anything, was white justice. Not the police, but the higher court system, which smiled fondly at the assailants because they were precious traditional men and regarded the victims as inconsequential casualties who'd just have to get over it.

It was in the main towns of the Northern Territory, up and down the highway, where most of the violence and abuse was happening daily, in full public view, and women and children were suffering most. The Northern Territory coroner, Greg Cavanagh, who reported late last year on the case of an Aboriginal man who did not get adequate medical assistance in Alice Springs hospital after being stabbed, said: "Alice Springs has the highest-reported incidence of stab wounds in the world. There were 1440 cases there in a seven-year period." Almost all those stabbings occurred in the Alice Springs town camps. The Territory's real sickness was routine urban adult slaughter, not remote child sex abuse.

Everyone knew that to make any headway on the real problem of Aboriginal violence, liquor supplies would have to be severely curtailed in the main towns. That was where Aborigines were buying alcohol. It wasn't available in the bush except under limited circumstances, in a handful of clubs or wet-canteens, which had strict six-can drinking or take-away limits. But no self-respecting white person was going to stand for full-on liquor restrictions, not in the Territory and not anywhere. Even on Aboriginal land, where it was more or less already banned, there were obstacles: white punters might in certain cases need to traverse Aboriginal land with an esky full of tinnies to go fishing. And the busloads of Dutch, Germans and Japanese would no longer be entitled to enjoy their complimentary tour-bus glass of champagne while watching the Uluru sunset. The emergency-response laws would initially outlaw all alcohol on all Aboriginal lands, but it was soon realised that this would affect some profitable and important tourist trade and the necessary non-indigenous drinking exemptions were provided.

The intervention, when announced, caught everyone off-guard. No one really expected it. As far as I'm aware, there were no pre-emptive leaks to preferred journalists. As for Brough, he should have gone to a Northern Territory bush community to announce the intervention, to stand on the dirt and tell his story. But he didn't. He stayed in the south, working the big-city radio stations. It was all about raped and defiled bush children. Whether they needed it or not, they were to be the emergency. Sex, good or bad, sold.

If the statistics told you that you, as an Aboriginal man, were going to be dead by forty or fifty, you too might live your short life in a series of extremes, sucking it all in, spewing it all out, knowing no such thing as abstinence or restraint, but with a determination to know every possible sexual, alcoholic or drug-induced excess to counter those times – and anyone who'd passed through a small Queensland or Territory or Western Australian town had seen it of Aboriginal men – when you were sitting down, doing long stretches of exactly nothing.

As a political tool, the Aboriginal emergency didn't work for John Howard or Mal Brough. Both men lost their seats on 24 November 2007. The intervention had little to do with either man's loss unless, in Brough's case, his electorate felt their high-profile federal member was too concerned with Aboriginal matters and not enough with local issues.

Those caring parts of the white population, forever sighing that "something" had to be done, were, initially, suspiciously welcoming of Brough. His words seemed to be cutting through years of inertia. Then they heard the permit system was to be lifted (albeit in a limited way), and that townships would be overtaken with forcibly acquired five-year leases. They heard about the compulsory health checks on Aboriginal children, and heard once again the fears of land and children being stolen. I'd like to think that at the very least they lost their nerve on 24 November 2007 and voted cautiously against the intervention. That didn't happen. The election was about new leadership and the ten- or eleven-year changing of the guard typical of the Australian electoral cycle. The intervention didn't appear on the radar. People just forgot about it altogether.

It had never been that Howard wanted to rescue Aborigines. He wanted to rescue himself. But that the intervention was to be one of his final, major acts, suggested he'd been prowling late about Kirribilli in his night-shirt, wondering what might move voters his way. He believed Aborigines might be a well-chosen topic. Howard realised there was a deep dissatisfaction about the state of Aboriginal Australia and he knew exasperated, well-to-do Australians held him accountable.

Howard said there was no politics in it – rather, it was the product of his belief that Aboriginal Australia had been allowed to run unchecked for too long. But to believe that, you would have to ignore his worst-ever stretch of bad polls – seven months of unremitting bad news. He'd been turning up for work but couldn't break through on any message. The emergency was about himself as much as anyone else. But who cared if it meant things were to change for the better?

Soon after the intervention was announced, I heard myself congratulating Howard, as though I were an on-air radio jock rather than a print reporter having a one-on-one interview down the phone line. But I'd long believed a radical adjustment was overdue, and the shock of the intervention announcement seemed worth something in itself. It appeared to be of the same order as Howard's post-Port Arthur gun laws and the 1999 East Timor liberation. "It's sort of in that category, yeah," Howard said. "I haven't preoccupied myself [with ranking it]. It's going to be a very tough thing. But it's an awful story."

Howard said it was up there with his most important work. "Yeah, I think I'm doing the right thing. I don't want to invest it with ego, but I really believe in it. It's one of those occasions in public life where you feel you can strike a decisive blow to make things better for a weak and vulnerable section of the community." I listened and wondered why he hadn't moved earlier. "We haven't changed our policy in relation to land rights generally," he continued. "But whatever is needed to be done in the process of establishing a safe society for indigenous children will be done. That is more important to me than anything else. It's more important than any doctrine or philosophy ... You just had that terrible running-on-the-spot feeling. You put a lot of effort and a lot of resources into the dysfunctional character of these communities. I watched what Noel Pearson was doing in the Cape and it made a lot of sense."

It was in 2003 when Howard first went in hard on Aborigines. He removed much funding control from the Aboriginal and Torres Strait Islander Commission, believing it dysfunctional and conflicted. He was deeply unhappy that ATSIC's regionally elected councillors continued to back chairman Geoff Clark, who was facing charges of rape and brawling, and that his deputy, Sugar Ray Robinson, was under investigation for fraud. It infuriated Howard that ATSIC's leadership saw themselves as an independent, albeit government-funded political clique, pushing rights agendas such as a treaty rather than setting forth down a path of practical apolitical administration which might lessen Aboriginal disadvantage. In 2005, Howard abolished ATSIC, a Labor creation, and re-assigned its few remaining areas of responsibility to various federal ministers. Howard wanted to mainstream all Aboriginal services, to end the administrative distinction between indigenous and non-indigenous Australians.

No Aboriginal community had been polled for its views, on anything, ever. It was not possible to say how they judged Howard for ending ATSIC. But he was also the no-Sorry man, the one who had offended so many by excising the coastal communities from the Australian mainland as part of the border control imperative, he was Liberal, he'd only visited the most easily accessible communities, and he was the one with the heeler ministers always nipping around the edges of the *Land Rights Act*. He was not loved in the bush, but that never bothered him. Aborigines had never voted for him. Six months out of the election he was chasing a grand gesture to assist his reinvention as a connected and compassionate guy. He wasn't hearing the thump of shovelled dirt on the coffins of the stabbed Aboriginal women; the unhappiness he sensed belonged to a white elite from both sides of politics, who felt it time that the wealthy country dealt with the stench coming from the far corner of the backyard.

Maybe such people had Rover Thomas or Emily Kngwarreye or John Mawurndjul paintings on their walls at home or in the boardroom. These were outlandishly accomplished examples of a culture's vibrancy and one did like to point them out to visitors and explain how this line of dots signified a certain serpent creation trail or how that squall of mad colour indicated a women's bush-potato site. Yet while such a piece may have been worth $125,000 at Sotheby's, it no longer seemed to have much to do with Aboriginal culture.

Anyone owning a valuable Aboriginal artwork might have wondered if they were admiring something that was no longer quite so real. An unrelenting press was now consistently documenting horrific stories from the north, and some of the major artists were occasional prison clients. These magnificent pieces, whoever their true author(s) were, were products of misery and were now hanging twisted on their walls. Investors were starting to hear how many of the high-priced paintings were being produced in the bullock-pen art slave sheds of Alice Springs – along with stories that some more famous Territory Aboriginal artists had not actually touched a brush to the paintings that bore their signatures, but had got their kids or clan relations to do the work while they were on extended drinking benders in the Todd River. It was like owning Nazi memorabilia. There were honourable galleries, but all now sold paintings with a back-up series of photos proving that the artist had been physically seated at his or her canvas. Art buyers loved the idea of blackfellas but didn't trust them as far as they could spit. Aboriginal art remained valuable, but buyers needed constant reassurance. If these works were to have their real value restored, the society that gave rise to them had to be addressed and corrected.

Howard had in 2002 begun assigning senior ministers to take special interest in certain areas, such as Port Keats (or Wadeye, as white people called it) and Cape York, where there were to be whole-of-government trials and where rich business people would also be enticed to show interest. Generous types were taken to meet Noel Pearson and left feeling confident that here was an Aboriginal leader who was talking the right way. He was deadly serious, deadly sober, and was not into exploiting white guilt but white opportunity. He had created a framework of ideas which was always three steps ahead of everyone else's and he'd mobilised young Aborigines by getting them involved in all kinds of projects. In other places, Howard's trials fell apart. It seemed Pearson was the only black man standing. He became a major force, writing short essays that defied easy translation unless you sat down and considered them very closely – though it was when he wrote or spoke from personal experience of seeing his own people's children cowering unfed in bush hovels that he was at his most eloquent and effective. In the Territory, and in the south, urban Aborigines came to resent Pearson's influence and to see him as a traitor to the leftist ideology Aborigines were expected to cling to. Whether Pearson wanted it or not, he had become the person whom the national leaders looked to for guidance. He was more than happy to lift up the rusty strip of corrugated iron and show everyone the resident snake beneath. He took up the crown as unmotivated Aborigines stewed in their own inactivity or ineffectiveness. Despite Howard appointing Aboriginal leaders to a national round-table advisory board, Pearson was the only Aborigine the government took seriously.

There was high-level jealousy business afoot. An '80s bumper-sticker had it that Aborigines were "One Voice, One Nation." It was a good line, but it didn't reflect how Aborigines saw themselves. They had always been many nations, distinct and disparate groups who shared the injury of colonisation but lived different lives, with different customs and different problems. What Pearson had again exposed, unwittingly, was that the Northern Territory, with a population of more tribal people than any other state in the nation, had no one to speak for it.

For Howard, it was always going to be too late to show that he cared. Perhaps he never really got over the way Aborigines stood and turned their backs on him for his refusal to say Sorry, and had allowed himself to become aggravated by the shrieking urban Aboriginal voice. He never thought to outsmart this group by seeking an alliance with a handful of impressive senior bush people from, say, north-east Arnhem Land. For his insights he relied on Pearson's writing, and his Aboriginal Affairs ministers. The first one he really trusted and loved was Brough. Brough was different. Howard saw him as his political son.

And Brough really did care, in his drill-sergeant way. Ever since being sworn in as minister in January 2006, he'd been on an intense mission to visit northern communities, where he didn't just listen with a polite, impatient frown – he ranted and swore. Paternalism these people well understood, so they more or less got Brough. They were just a little taken aback by his delivery.

Aborigines could evict almost everyone else from their land, but land-rights legislation gave Brough, like any other federal or Territory politician, special dispensation to enter their world whenever he wished. The rest of Australia was shut out, just as Aboriginal residents were shut in. Sometimes Brough took the press with him; sometimes he didn't. He never looked much at home with Aboriginal men. He was a ladies' man. But one thing everyone had to admit: he was at least turning up, in person, for a look.

In April 2006, Brough was in Port Keats where he saw firsthand the town's clan-based gangs, the Evil Warriors, assembling in the streets as they prepared to face off against the enemy, Judas Priest. He couldn't believe it. It had been written about, but he was seeing it. "I'm the man from Canberra," he screamed, as the only reporter on the scene, the Bulletin's Adam Shand, took notes. "I control all the bloody money that comes in here for Centrelink … If you boys go over the hill tonight to fight those guys, I will cut your money off. Do you fucking well understand what I'm saying?" Go Mal. It was not possible to imagine previous Aboriginal Affairs ministers, such as Kay Patterson, Amanda Vanstone, Philip Ruddock, John Herron, Robert Tickner, Gerry Hand or Clyde Holding, standing in the midst of a warrior dust-up and telling them to get their act together. The warmongers shuffled, looked embarrassed and laid down their arms. The Keats police had never seen such a thing; the last time they'd commanded such control of a situation was when one of their sergeants shot a boy dead with his Glock pistol. Brough got them right where it hurt: the money.

Passion and outrage were Mal's weapons. And he used them most decisively on the Northern Territory government. The national press, led by the *Australian* and the *Bulletin*, had been hammering the Territory Labor government, hard, for years. By 2006, the ABC's *Lateline* had joined in, citing the frustration of the Alice Springs crown prosecutor, Dr Nanette Rogers, at ongoing brutality against women and children. Rogers had given a speech a month earlier, talking about cases that had already been dealt with by the courts. It was not new but, as sometimes happens with certain stories, the stars aligned in *Lateline*'s favour. It took off.

Things may not have been worse than they ever were, but nor were they better. And the media was no longer producing stories and watching them dissipate. The spinifex was alight. The homicide rates were unceasing, the Aborigine-on-Aborigine horrific sexual assaults were routinely horrific, and the imprisonment rates of Aboriginal men were higher than ever. On this last point, Northern Territory Labor brandished the statistics not as a matter of shame but of pride: it showed the local white voters that they were tough on crime. But nationally, Territory Labor was hurting. Indigenous life was not improving under their watch. Women – and therefore children – were as vulnerable as ever.

When Clare Martin was elected as Labor chief minister of the Northern Territory, even to her own surprise, in 2001 after twenty-seven years of Country Liberal Party rule, people celebrated the fall of a party that had been there too long and had become hard and arrogant. Most of those who voted Labor did so not for the sake of social justice for Aborigines but simply because Martin, a former journalist, appeared professional and unthreatening. Democracy had become unhealthy in the north: change for the sake of change was needed. The CLP's chief minister, Denis Burke, a former brigade commander, was a nice enough bloke with some deeply shallow views. Upon Labor's victory, even the Territory's first-ever chief minister, the CLP's Paul Everingham, turned up in Darwin to congratulate the new government and wonder why it had taken everyone so long to do their duty as citizens.

Another significant group – I will not call them "intellectuals" but "the worried" – voted NT Labor partly because they would have done so regardless, but also with the hope and certain belief that Martin would launch a mission to make up for the lost years and bring Aborigines aboard the mothership. It was tiring and maddening the way bush Aborigines were seen as some sort of disease that whites might contract. During election campaigns, the Country Liberal Party had two trusty old tricks: to promote images of nasty prisoners who would all be set free under limp-wristed Labor; and its standard fallback terror tactic – that Aborigines were organising and coming to take what was yours, White Man.

Anyone who cared to open their front door and look out could see that was not going to happen. Aborigines were on the streets of Darwin, Katherine, Mataranka, Elliott, Borroloola, Tennant Creek and Alice Springs, the men stumbling drunk and the women stumbling drunk too, though they had swollen bottom lips and cliff-edge eye sockets from all the punching. These people a threat?

People could not understand why it was that Aboriginal children were wandering about communities with cans of petrol stuck to their faces. The rawness of this form of self-harm was deeply confronting. And why was it that agencies which should have been working in backstreets in Calcutta or in the Sudan or Rwanda, such as World Vision and Mother Teresa's Sisters of Charity, were positioned on the Northern Territory's Aboriginal frontline? It didn't fit with how coastal city people saw their Australia. By 2001, Howard was deep into his own ruthlessly creative and successful border-control measures. It was those who might come, not those who already lived here, who mattered most.

When Martin won, there was an expectation that she would want to, surely, finally, pull the frame into focus, even though the task would be immense. Territory Labor had inherited three decades of CLP apathy and neglect. In many communities, people were living or trying to work in buildings that pre-dated Territory self-government in 1978. They'd been built back in the late '60s and were falling down, not just because of rampaging wild boys but because of age and lack of maintenance. The CLP saw no need to address these basic infrastructure problems: Aborigines were Aborigines – and they were Labor voters. Big public money was directed to stadiums, resorts, entertainment centres, convention centres and hotels. The bush had been left to rot.

Much of newspaper-reading Australia had been sickened by the injustice of the CLP's mandatory sentencing, which was seeing third-strike offenders sent to jail for twelve months for minuscule offences – such as Jamie Wurramurra, banished to Berrimah Prison for stealing biscuits and cordial from a Groote Eylandt mine site office on Christmas Day. In some ways, Aborigines found it easier to accept mandatory sentencing than others. Although reliable Labor voters, they were often deeply conservative people who believed in swift, clean justice. The threat of prison had always worked as a deterrent to white people because they saw it as about the worst thing that could happen: a jail sentence raised a real chance of being bashed or raped. Yet so many young Aboriginal men knew the inside of jail. You would often hear know-all white people claiming it was a rite of passage for Aborigines, particularly for the tough men of Groote Eylandt, Port Keats and the vast Warlpiri nation. I had been pleased to get the first-ever interview with the mysterious, charismatic and – as it turned out – irrationally feared John Shelvey Kurungaiyi, leader of the Evil Warriors gang (he said "not gang, it's just family") in Berrimah jail. When I put the "rite-of-passage" question to him, he looked at me as if I was out of my mind. Did I seriously think he wanted to be in jail? He was doing time for assault, not charged under mandatory sentencing, and explained that he had a baby on the outside that he had not yet met. The idea of Aborigines liking prison was absurd to him. He didn't want to be a prison leader, which he was; he wanted to be home in his community. It was true that tribal Aborigines could enjoy protection and do relatively easy prison time. But this didn't mean a law aimed at sending Aborigines to prison was right.

Martin's first legislative act was promising: she kept her word and removed the wicked mandatory sentencing laws. It was celebrated as a seismic settling correction. Martin's first symbolic act was to keep to her word and provide a Sorry to the Territory's stolen generations. This was when reporters first sensed there was something up with Martin. And it was – as it would be for the next six years of her leadership – rather akin to that feeling you get after take-off from Sydney heading north to Darwin: you hit one of those clashing headwind vortexes and the plane seems to be not flying, but falling, or frighteningly motionless. If you were lucky, the captain would come on and explain the sensation you were experiencing was "perfectly normal" and "nothing to worry about" and you'd try to relax and cleave to your faith in science.

Media minders showed journalists a copy of the apology Martin proposed to read to the legislative assembly; it was noticed that she was not going to use the word "Sorry" in her apology. It didn't matter what your personal views on the whole Sorry debacle-distraction were; what mattered was that she had said she was going to say it and now she wasn't. She was going to do exactly what Howard had done and offer an expression of generic regret. Busloads were arriving in Darwin for the great moment. When they were told that Sorry hadn't made the final cut, there was disbelief, then outrage. Martin and her people had failed to grasp years of national debate. Setting aside people's feelings, the whole thing was about semantics, and the semantics required you say Sorry. A hasty press conference was called and Martin announced it had been an unfortunate oversight. Of course she would say Sorry.

Behind so much of what would become Martin's unwillingness to act on Aboriginal issues was Paul Tyrrell. Tyrrell had been head of the chief minister's department under the CLP. Instead of booting him out and getting her own CEO, Martin kept Tyrrell on. It baffled and infuriated her party. Tyrrell had been the CLP's oil, gas and general big-development urger. He was an old-fashioned bureaucrat whose first instinct was to keep a government out of trouble, rather than govern. And if something became hard to handle, his attitude was: it'll blow over.

If, as suspected, Martin got her political education from *Yes, Minister*, then she missed the message: while Sir Humphrey's knowledge was useful, in the end it was always her call. But Martin was deeply insecure on business matters and allowed Tyrrell to be her sole policy guide. Martin decided to manage rather than govern, and Territory Labor took control with a virtually unaltered CLP mentality. It appeared that Tyrrell's message to Martin was to remember that it was the white voters of Darwin's northern suburbs that had given her power; and while the Aboriginal bush seats had kept her party alive through the long opposition years, there was nothing to be gained from rewarding their loyalty.

Martin kept the Indigenous Affairs portfolio to herself, among many others, and promptly set about doing nothing with it. It was deliberate. The Darwin population was so often presented to the world as a warmly multicultural mob, but all that really meant was that we had outdoor markets that sold noodles. The redneck sentiment still ran deep — always had and always would. The white urban population was showing signs of growing and Darwin real estate was becoming worth something, with land and housing prices comparable to Perth and Sydney. People did not want Labor running some sort of black agenda.

Yet the northern capital was still the frontier. Families, many of them connected with Defence or behind the great rush to build the hideous stands of apartment towers that were disfiguring the skyline, would arrive on short contracts. Your kids would get to know their kids and a few birthday parties later they were gone forever. The voting intentions of this mobile crowd were somewhat mysterious but seen as important. They spent money on eight-seater Land Cruiser wagons and bought dinghies and trailers and briefly enjoyed the famous Territory lifestyle of barra hunting and big-crocodile spotting. There was finally a real sense of prosperity in the north and few stopped to wonder why there were ever-greater numbers of aimless black people staggering about the streets. They were seen as drunken bludgers. And that was right, in a passing snapshot way. People were starting to beg openly on the streets, which was new.

John Ah Kit, a long-time Aboriginal Labor politician, in his first term as a Territory government minister, gave a brutally honest speech about his frustration at being hit up by his countrymen for cash outside his local fish and chip shop. He let it be known it was time everyone had a good, long talk. But there was a leadership bottleneck: Martin was interested in the fish, not the chips. Her only stated vision was to build more boat ramps to get more white people with dinghies into the water. Martin believed the people she had to keep closest were these, the fishing and V8 Supercar crowd – and, indeed, history showed she was attending a Super-car function on the June 2007 day when Mal Brough announced the fed-eral intervention. She had her head down in a high-octane donk and didn't see it coming. Nor had she guarded her back from her own party.

There had been deep disquiet at her total non-handling of Aboriginal matters. The Territory was running to a near 30 per cent Aboriginal pop-ulation and, with infant mortality now under control (thanks, I would contend, to the lovely, fattening, life-sustaining and life-shortening deep-fried chicken available in the bain-marie of every single community store, but that's another thesis for another day), it was the bush where numbers were growing fastest. There were now five Aboriginal Labor parliamen-tarians – the most ever, anywhere, in the nation's history. They wanted action but Martin wasn't listening to them, or to her senior policy staff, who were anxious for her to reveal a plan to tackle overcrowding in Abo-riginal housing, to address bad kidney and rheumatic hearts and the sniffer kids and chronic alcoholism and, most of all, to address education and domestic violence. There was a strong sense that Martin needed to outline a vision which showed she wanted to take the Aboriginal popula-tion with her. She declined.

On 1 June 2006, Matthew Bonson, the member for Millner, from an old Darwin Aboriginal family, sent an email to his four Aboriginal parliamentary colleagues and to two senior non-indigenous ministers, Paul Henderson and the deputy chief minister, Syd Stirling. The document, titled "Notes relating to Bulletin Magazine articles," was leaked. Bonson's memo referred to two articles I had written. One of them was an open attack on Martin's failure to embrace – let alone discuss – Aboriginal matters, and suggested she ought to relinquish her Indigenous Affairs portfolio to a minister who might make better use of it. The other story was about nasty ongoing violence in the Bagot community, a town camp located right in the middle of Darwin, on a busy main road, and in Bonson's electorate. The general message was that if the government couldn't lift from the swill those in front of their very eyes, those in the bush had no hope.

Bonson complained Martin was doing nothing. It was time for her to give up the portfolio. He wrote: "In the last two weeks, speaking with local community people and hearing general comment, I am concerned at the level of misunderstanding and even hate toward the chief minister."

Bonson was duly sent out to face the media, saying his memo was just an unfortunate "brain explosion," but the rat was halfway out of the cage. In mid-June 2006, Martin foolishly chose not to attend a summit Brough had called to look into general abuse in Aboriginal communities and towns. She sent a junior ministerial delegation in her place. Brough filed the insult in his top drawer. Meanwhile, *Lateline* was reporting allegations of central Australian Aboriginal men keeping child petrol-sniffers as their sex slaves. Brough joined in, and extrapolated, claiming there were entrenched paedophile networks in central Australian communities.

The Australian Crime Commission was instructed to set up a task-force in Alice Springs to get to the bottom of the sexual exploitation of children. The ACC was used to dealing with organised criminals and relied on electronic surveillance and coercive powers to compel witnesses to answer questions at secret hearings. Such methods were not going to work in central Australia, as they well knew; listening in on bugged phones to people communicating in Pitjantjatjara wasn't going to tell them much. They trod softly and heard some terrible stories, but they related to opportunistic, individual sex fiends who happened to be black.

Brough seemed certain he'd find a paedophile under every outback rock. He talked recklessly of extant "rings," implying there was a degree of sophistication in the bush – images circulating on computers, or ritualistic gatherings at which children were sexually sacrificed. They did not exist. But Aboriginal child-sex offenders did, of course, and they were hard to get at. As men, they held the political power in their communities, and shared with other men cultural networks across the lands which were privileged and secret and which excluded women. Women and children were silent and powerless, rarely able to call upon the wider, collective support of Aboriginal men when serious individual offenders were operating in their midst.

Because of this, trying to get Aboriginal women and children to talk was hard going. The Australian Crime Commission could, and often would, use its powers to jail a bikie for refusing to talk, but jailing Aboriginal victims for their silence would obviously be counter-productive. The central Australian Aboriginal women's violence group, Ngaanyatjarra Pitjantjatjara Yankunytjatjara, or NPY, had been closely monitoring and helping expose individual cases of abuse. They had eyes and ears all over the central Australian bush and, knowing that perpetrators were highly mobile, played a significant role in convincing Territory, Western Australian and South Australian police to link arms in cross-border policing. NPY was seen by some as right-wing for its willingness to expose abuse. It wasn't. It simply took the view – in Australia, a revolutionary one – that it did not care that the assailant might be a traditional man. Victims would come first.

The policing of general Aboriginal violence was never easy for lower-ranking officers. There was the usual mix of junior copper deadshits with lazy-brained ideas about Aborigines, and those who tried but found their work frustrating. They would often work to help a badly beaten woman only to find she wouldn't co-operate in pressing charges and, upon release from hospital, could be found drinking with the man who'd bashed her. There was an understandably cynical view that it was all a waste of time, but the Territory police commissioner, Paul White, elevated some impressive women cops to supervisory ranks and made it clear that stopping abuse against Aboriginal women and children was one of his priorities. Police began entering town camps hunting down men for domestic violence breaches.

Martin's advisers – the ones she wasn't listening to – were uneasy. The federal government was starting to take an interest in Aborigines as never before. Up to this point the role of successive federal Aboriginal Affairs ministers had more or less been to sign off on the recommendations of Aboriginal land commissioners and grant tracts of land to traditional owners.

Mal Brough was a very different creature. By the time he had been appointed to the portfolio, in the early 2006 reshuffle, the Coalition had control of the Senate. Real change was possible. And if you thought about what he got up to in less than two years, few federal ministers, in any portfolio, could lay claim to having such a wild, intense ride. Before the intervention was announced, Brough made himself known to the Territory on four key points: town camps, 99-year leases for townships, remote-area housing and the permit system. These were his early mini-interventions, and it is necessary to examine them because they help explain the philosophy, or lack of it, behind his later national emergency response.

At Brough's first meeting with Martin, in early 2006, it was she who raised the problem of town camps – particularly the eighteen or so small humpy towns of Alice Springs, which took quaint names like Little Sisters or Old Timers or Trucking Yards. Brough's people claimed it was she who asked Brough for help, admitting her government could not handle the issues of violence and atrocious housing. Fair enough. Brough made the point that he did not have responsibility for the town camps. While populated exclusively by Aborigines, they were not on Aboriginal land; they were special-purpose leases owned by the Territory government, and which the Territory could compulsorily acquire if it so desired. In March 2007, Brough put $60 million on the table to upgrade the camps, on the condition the Territory government took back control of its leases from the various town camps which were under the umbrella control of the Aboriginal-run Tangentyere Council, and transformed the camps into normal Alice Springs suburbs, with Territory Housing taking responsibility for housing and the council providing standard servicing. The housing associations and Tangentyere had, by any reasonable measure, failed in their role of managing the camps. (Tangentyere would argue it had never been properly funded.)

According to an essay by the executive director of Tangentyere, William Tilmouth, in a 2007 anti-intervention collection of essays called *Coercive Reconciliation*, the town camps had been created around the outskirts of Alice Springs as a result of a law that prohibited Aborigines being in town after dark. They congregated in traditional camping and ceremonial fringe areas along tribal lines. The 1968 NT Cattle Station Industry Award arrived, requiring Aboriginal stockmen be paid equal wages, which led to more and more bush people moving to town and full-time unemployment. Tangentyere was able to negotiate special-purpose leases on the camps and, through the years of occupancy, had come to regard the camps as Aboriginal land — which they were in appearance, though not in law. On 18 April 2007, two months before the intervention, Tangentyere held a meeting of town-camp residents, who resolved to refuse Brough's offer for upgrades in return for surrendering their leases. In Tilmouth's essay, "Saying No to $60 Million," he referred to bad housing and general unhygienic conditions but never once to the violence of the camps, which had become a national disgrace.

The Territory could have overridden Tangentyere in a flash but couldn't bring itself to support Brough's proposal: it believed it would have to pay just terms and compensation for resuming the leases, and could only see political grief in ending the reign of a major grassroots Aboriginal organisation. Some of the town-camp dwellers were permanent, but many were transients who came in from bush and crashed at the camps. Either way, they were all connected to the bush and all were Labor voters. The Territory government was incapable of acting. The deal lost traction and fell through. Brough would regard the failure to seal a deal on town camps as his greatest disappointment as minister.

Brough's second pre-intervention measure targeted woeful housing. The Commonwealth funded indigenous housing through a surviving remnant of ATSIC. It was known as the Community Housing Infrastructure Program (CHIP), and put money into state and territory pools. The states and the Territory were then supposed to match the federal funds dollar-for-dollar. The Territory, according to the federal government, was lagging badly. Trashed houses and overcrowding were one of the pillars of dysfunction so, in one of its first attempts to get across their new portfolio, the Brough team sat around trying to figure out who owned remote-area housing and who was responsible for its maintenance. It quickly formed a view that the Commonwealth neither owned, nor was legally responsible for, remote housing. Through CHIP, remote-area housing had been "gifted" to Indigenous Community Housing Organisations, known as ICHOs. The ICHOs built or refurbished houses, and thereafter their responsibility appeared to cease. They had no one to answer to and did not appear to regard their housing stock as an asset, but as something inevitably doomed for destruction. The expectation was that if a house was trashed, it would be refurbished at public cost. Government policy did not seem to work this way in respect of any other public assets, except perhaps a tank that took a hit in a war zone. Brough also believed that opportunities for nepotism – the way ICHOs could preferentially allocate housing to big men and their mates – were too freely available under this system.

Brough ordered a survey of CHIP by PriceWaterhouseCoopers: as expected, the report came back saying CHIP was failing Aborigines. Brough went to Cabinet saying something had to change. He wanted Aborigines in eastern costal communities removed from CHIP and dealt with as ordinary, mainstream, housing-commission clients. He proposed the Australian Remote Indigenous Accommodation (ARIA) program and got the blessing of Cabinet to negotiate with the states and the Territory. The major effect of ARIA was to concentrate housing spending on remote areas.

Brough was not prepared to build new houses only to consign them to destruction. Wherever possible, where new houses were to be built on Aboriginal land, he wanted new land-tenure arrangements which would turn communities into normal towns. This, he reasoned, would allow businesses to get moving in the townships and would better protect the Commonwealth's investments. Thus arose the third of Brough's major pre-intervention initiatives: 99-year leases. It was, in fact, an idea conceived by the Territory government, which was likewise frustrated by communal Aboriginal housing organisations and the lack of development within Aboriginal towns. Because Aboriginal land could never be bought or sold, banks were reluctant to lend to enterprises for Aboriginal land – they could never call in an asset.

Under the Brough plan, public housing would be controlled by the Territory housing commission; so when a house was trashed in Nguiu, for instance, the tenants would be dealt with like any other housing-commission client. These clients would also, for the first time, have the opportunity to rent-buy their houses, at cheap loan rates. This, it was hoped, would see Aborigines not only taking greater responsibility for their homes, but also being able to enter the housing market. The great Australian dream, as Brough saw it, was heading bush.

Under Brough, the Land Rights Act was amended in 2006 to allow for the 99-year leases. The newly inserted section 19A provided that traditional owners could agree to grant a 99-year head lease over a township to a government entity. That entity would act almost as a real estate agent, and would encourage economic development by granting sub-leases within the town area to outside commercial interests and governments seeking to build infrastructure.

Traditional owners who signed up would be paid rent for the use of their land, in some cases for the first time, and would allow their towns to become public, with no permit required to enter. Any proposed commercial enterprise would need to satisfy the proper-purpose requirements outlined in the head lease, which sought to prevent – for example – inappropriate high-rise or creek-polluting factories. But once the traditional owners signed, they would have no control over development within the township area covered by the head lease.

Brough was working hard on several communities – on Groote Eylandt, Elcho Island, the Tiwi Islands and in Port Keats – to get the traditional owners to sign up to 99-year leases. The government was turning up to talk to traditional owners holding satellite photos of the proposed town-lease areas. They basically drew big circles around existing towns. They wanted it all, including cemeteries, barge landings and outlying gravel pits. The government didn't want a situation whereby bits and pieces of a town were not part of the 99-year head lease; this did not fit with Brough's all-or-nothing ideology and would make for messy administration, with people forced to tiptoe around those public areas of town which might be closed.

The Northern Territory government agreed in principle with 99-year leases but was arguing that an Aboriginal land trust, rather than the government, should control the head lease. But the problem, as the Commonwealth and the Northern Land Council agreed, was that while an Aboriginal town might have a population of 1000, there were, in some cases, only four or five actual traditional owners. Most of the population had their traditional lands in the wider region and did not speak for the land on which towns were located. For the lease to be genuinely beneficial to a community, it could not be held in the names of a few traditional owners: this would give them too much power over other local Aborigines, possibly turn them into slum landlords, and might see them trying to dishonour the terms of the lease by trying to interfere with outsiders wanting to start businesses.

Brough was insistent: traditional owners would lease back whole zoned township areas, for a fee, to an arm's-length holding entity. The entity had to be a responsible organisation – probably formed out of an existing local housing organisation or a local council, with traditional owners and independent outsiders sitting as board members. The controlling head lease would reside in the name of a faceless, disinterested Canberra bureaucrat.

It was up to the traditional owners to agree to the terms of any 99-year lease. No town had to sign, but it became clear that those who did would receive preferential treatment when it came to receiving money for housing and infrastructure. Some called it a land grab, but Aborigines would not lose the underlying tenure to their land; they would commit it elsewhere for a few decades.

There was talk that Brough was blackmailing the people of Nguiu, on the Tiwi Islands, north of Darwin, that if they didn't sign a 99-year lease they wouldn't get the on-island boarding school they so dearly wanted for their kids. In the end, Nguiu signed. By the time Brough ended his reign as minister, Nguiu was the only town that had.

Brough had meanwhile taken a special interest in Port Keats because he regarded it as a horror zone. But he'd found his ideology challenged on whether or not outstations should be permitted to continue to exist. The view of a former Liberal minister, Amanda Vanstone, had been that outstations – small groups of semi-permanently occupied houses located in the bush on a clan group's land – were "cultural museums." (An Aboriginal man, Peter Danaga, from western Arnhem Land, offered a clever retort to this. We were at the Ji-malawa outstation, east of Maningrida, where two elderly women were fashioning fish traps from pandanus. Danaga told me: "It's true my old ladies are a museum. They are full of knowledge. And they are passing that knowledge on. Out here is a big backyard, full of knowledge and information. That's what museums are, aren't they?")

Vanstone's view was that outstations were places where Aborigines indulged themselves, tinkering around, doing pretty much bugger-all, maybe starting a lawnmower once a month, maybe unravelling the odd canvas and doing a bit of art, or maybe tearing a few pandanus strands through their teeth to make woven baskets or floor mats and god knew what else. They were getting paid CDEP or the dole and, more than likely, not sending their kids to school. Vanstone wanted these people to give up this life and come into the bigger townships.

Brough was initially of the Vanstone view. But in Port Keats he found families desperate to escape the trouble in town and reside permanently at their outstations. If he, on the one hand, was describing Keats as a hell-hole, then he had to regard those parents who wanted to extricate their kids and live in outstations as perfectly rational. He decided he was pre-pared to support outstations, so long as they were close enough to town-ships that children could get to school every day, and to a clinic if they needed one. He made what he called a down payment of good faith and supported the little Wadapuli and Namar outstations in the building of twenty new houses. Under the plan, residents would pay $150 rent per week and had to school their children regularly. If they met these condi-tions, they could, after two years, buy their homes cheaply on a subsi-dised loan scheme.

At least that was what Brough told the media. It wasn't true. The Aborig-inal land trust had agreed to head lease the land to the government's Indigenous Business Australia, which built the houses. The IBA became the landlord, sub-leasing the land back to the Aboriginal tenants. They would never own their homes; they were public-housing tenants and that's all they would ever be.

And even if they did have the opportunity to buy these homes, the idea of them entering the housing market was absurd. The many clans of the

Keats region would only ever live on their own clan estates. A Port Keats family from an outstation in the coastal Treachery Bay area south of town would never seek to buy or trade-up into housing on land belonging to river people from the north. It would be unthinkable. The Wadapuli people were charmed by Brough and his people, but what investment had they really made? Their children would one day inherit outstation homes that could never be traded. The notion that these people were entering the housing market was completely false. Still, they'd got new homes out of Brough and I like to think of it this way: they conned each other.

The Northern Land Council watched – and participated – with great interest. And, surprisingly, it didn't seem too stressed. It knew that Brough wanted 99-year leases, but it also knew traditional owners didn't have to sign. What, it reasoned, was the Commonwealth going to do? Would it really punish communities who hadn't signed by not building them new houses, schools or clinics? Unlikely. If the traditional owners the NLC represented insisted on signing on to 99-year leases, it would help. But it wasn't spruiking the concept, trying to get people to sign. It knew a federal election was coming.

After the intervention was announced, the Northern Land Council remained broadly supportive of the measures, though observers and critics couldn't see why. But the NLC knew the time was coming for big change in regards to town land, whether under the Coalition or Labor; the Commonwealth had long since run out of patience for spending money building on unsecured land. The NLC also knew that the pre-existing section 19 of the *Land Rights Act* already allowed for parts of a town to be sub-leased anyway. It sensed that whoever was in power, great opportunity was coming to the north.

Most of all, it knew that Brough had stolen $700–800 million from the states for stage two of his intervention, which was the rebuilding phase. It was more money than either the Territory government or the NLC had ever imagined. The NLC knew Labor had given its commitment to much of the Brough package. The NLC wanted to be there to help spend it.

Brough was by now stalking the north with a four-by-two. He was using federal powers to intervene on Territory turf with the Australian Crime Commission, housing, 99-year leases and town camps. Clare Martin needed to show at least passing interest in addressing abuse and neglect in the Aboriginal communities, lest Brough decided to awaken even more intrusive powers. And because the Territory was not a fully fledged state, Martin knew he could do it. The Northern Land Council, once upon a time an NT Labor ally, had bypassed the Territory government and was dealing directly with the federal government on the matter of the national nuclear waste dump, which South Australia had used its state powers to reject. The NLC had found a group of traditional owners from Muckaty station, north of Tennant Creek, who said they were prepared to build the thing on their land, for a price. The federal government was naturally delighted with the idea that Aborigines were coming to them wanting to embrace such a contentious issue. It seemed to suggest Aborigines were perhaps not stick-in-the-mud Labor types after all. But the Muckaty dump plan showed, if anything, how desperate Aborigines had become. If they had reasonable incomes and reasonable prospects, like the people of Nedlands or Toorak or Fannie Bay or Glenelg, they would never have gone near a dump. It also meant that Martin, and the Territory, was now exposed on all flanks.

High levels of sexually transmitted disease in communities were attracting attention. There was nothing new in this: STD rates, and promiscuity, had always been red-lining in the bush. The federal government latched onto it as a marker of the failure of the Territory government, but it didn't necessarily follow that children were being constantly and indiscriminately raped. What appeared to be happening was that sexually active teenagers were not seeking treatment for their STDs. They would continually pass disease back and forwards among each other. It was, more than anything, a health-education issue for teenagers, same as anywhere else in the world. The real miracle was that HIV hadn't taken hold.

Brough's office knew there were some horrific police actions underway – most noticeably the 2006 allegations that seven boys and men had repeatedly raped an eleven-year-old boy at Maningrida. The case was a perfect example of the sickness pervading Aboriginal Australia. It involved pornographic DVDs; ganja; anal penetration; hog-tying of the victim; and there were adults in the next room of one of the houses when one of the many assaults on the boy was said to have occurred. This was homosexual gang-rape. How could that happen?

In 2006, I was summoned to Maningrida by senior people to discuss the gang-sex case. They wanted it known that homosexual gang-rape had no place, or precedent, in their culture. I thought: okay. But with this tradition of old men taking the young women for themselves – a tradition on the wane – you sometimes wondered if teenage boys had sex with each other as a matter of necessity. It was well documented that it happened in nearby Irian Jaya. But you had to take people at their word. They wanted it known that they were not blasé about the event; that they were trying to deal with what had happened.

When the first case broke, I rang a mate in Maningrida. He said: "This is terrible for Maningrida." I said to him: "No. It's terrible for the boy who it happened to." He rang back later and said, "What you said is right. It's just very disappointing that it has happened." What he was concerned about was Brough, who was intensely interested in the case and had been referring to it in parliamentary speeches. No doubt the case bothered him; it would have bothered anyone. But there was the sense that Brough was shopping about Aboriginal Australia for a tragedy that would help him sell his politics.

The senior people were likewise worried Brough would find some way to make Maningrida pay. There was the usual talk about tough law, but where was tough law when the boy was being raped over a period of months? It was clear that enough adults in the town had known it was happening.

I tried to get a sense of whether they cared for the victim, which they said they did, but they seemed more concerned about what it said about their society as a whole. This was ultimately a mature, political approach – the actual event might have been shocking, but it was their role to think about the deeper ramifications. They said what they needed most of all was help: they didn't want to lose control. They wanted the best white lawyers and judges to come to Maningrida to help them deal with their problems. I reported that. No one came. Least of all Mal Brough.

If you stood back, it was possible to see the boy's rape for what it really was: part *Lord of the Flies*, part opportunistic sex. It was about getting off, about overpowering a victim. These kids weren't gay. If they'd found a girl to dominate, as would soon be seen in the Aurukun case, that would have been even better. The behaviour was not cultural. It was learned from porn. That became clear when the police charge-sheet revealed that young boys, some barely pubescent, were wanking themselves while watching older boys penetrate the victim. Something was seriously wrong here: the assailants saw themselves as performers, which is what porn is all about. There was no sense of sexual privacy. They didn't mind performing in front of other boys. They wanted to see who could pull off the most heroic sexual performance. They were all, when you saw them in the Supreme Court dock, dismal little heroes. It seemed some were infantile to the point of not being able to achieve ejaculation. They were prodding sticks up the poor kid's anus because they didn't have the sexual wherewithal to do anything else. It was truly pathetic. It was an example of what small towns, which offer no exit route, could do to kids: they'd never be international superstars in any other field, so they might as well be sex superstars for each other in small-town Maningrida.

The emergency response would be marketed as a child-sex intervention, but it was clear the real emergency was parental neglect. Had there been more care and more concern, more monitoring of children, this would never have happened. It was unfortunate for Maningrida, which was probably the most functional large-scale community in the Top End. It had no bar or wet-canteen, but a very sensible binge-drinking policy.

The barge would arrive from Darwin every fortnight and people would either drink their small beer ration in one night or try hard to hide a few beers for the coming days. People would spend most of their time dead sober till the next barge arrived.

If you were one of those people who believed that no black person should be allowed a drink, ever, then good for you. Maybe you belonged in Iran, where your views were accepted wisdom. In drinking sessions I'd had with Aborigines, whites and Muslims, the question only ever arose about the drinker, not the drink. That may have been akin to the US gun lobby's argument that guns didn't kill people; people did. Whatever, the Maningrida child-rape case had nothing to do with alcohol, or even ganja: it was about the failure of the family system, with no one taking responsibility for kids; it was about arrogant fathers who'd encouraged their children to believe they were unanswerable to Australian law and only ever needed answer to Aboriginal law. Aborigines would often say it was whites who had changing laws, while theirs remained constant. It may have been true, but theirs were in bad need of either maintenance or enforcement.

Yet the Maningrida art shop was more or less magnificent, depending on what treasures had just come in from the outstations on any given day. There was no routine reports of murder or sexual assault (apart from the recent aberration) and there were all sorts of local businesses, run using CDEP employees, that seemed functional. You could get a tyre repaired in Maningrida during business hours. You could get fuel. And half-decent food. They were baking their own mud bricks for housing. The outstation lifestyle was alive and well; and the ranger program seemed to be world-class. They should have been paid full-time government wages for doing such important work. But the government funded them on CDEP, the same organisation it so dearly wanted to abolish.

Most Australians have never been to an Aboriginal community in the Northern Territory. Why would they? The signposts upon entry into Aboriginal land pointed to the dire consequences of having a bottle of wine in your car (you could lose the vehicle); you'd need a permit and a reason to be there, and there was nowhere to stay once you arrived. They might never encounter the slow-lighting fuse of Aboriginal warmth and humour, or discover that Aborigines did not represent the last vestiges of a doomed society but a living culture with some intriguing modern modifications. Aboriginal tradition might have been ancient, but the fact that it was still being used meant it was contemporary, too.

In Arnhem Land towns and outstations, people buried their loved ones in their backyards and covered the dirt graves with plastic flowers. Death was supposedly a very touchy subject among Aborigines. Yet there was Grandma, just inside the fence and six foot down, right in everyone's face. Delegations of representatives from communities near and far flew in on light planes to assist relatives in the burying of the dead, or to participate in the beautiful boys-to-men ceremonies; the teenage girls swayed through the night in neat lines to the beat-box music. Family groups lit fires on the sunset beach. And while the issue of overcrowding was real, some people would explain that they chose to live this way, fifteen to a house, in the same way that extended families slept close in bush campsites. The bush towns – even Port Keats, on a good day – seemed pretty functional to me, apart from the rubbish and the lack of government spending.

Nor would most Australians have seen the red-eyed kava drinkers with "crocodile" skin who didn't talk but jibbered; or the petrol-sniffer boys flitting about in the woodlands, publicly wanking themselves, having lost the part of the brain that governs inhibition. Yet, when seeing such things, you had to measure them against what was happening in your own neighbourhood. I lived on a main road in Darwin, in one of the supposedly "better" suburbs. It had an open-door loony bin (mostly white residents) and a single man's hostel (all white residents) near a primary school. There were clusters of housing-commission flats just off the main road, with many Aboriginal residents. The public drunkenness on nearby inner-suburban Parap Road, right outside Clare Martin's electorate office, was borderline anarchy. Women were prostituting themselves for liquor.

Across town, two children could be regularly found begging for money outside the Darwin cinemas.

Following the 2006 *Lateline* report of children being used as sex slaves, Clare Martin ordered the police into Mutitjulu in the centre for an intense sweep of the community. The police raid uncovered nothing, but pressure on Martin continued to mount. She was at last persuaded by her advisers to act: she announced an inquiry into child sex abuse in Aboriginal communities, to be headed by Darwin Aboriginal woman Pat Anderson, known for her work in Aboriginal health, and Rex Wild, QC, the just-retired Director of Public Prosecutions. The key point in the inquiry's terms of reference was: "Examine the extent, nature and factors contributing to the sexual abuse of Aboriginal children, with a particular focus on unreported incidents of such abuse."

In announcing her inquiry, Martin, it appeared, had grown up to the extent that she was now prepared to order the royal commission-type investigation that responsible governments sometimes had to face up to. But the selection of Wild as co-chair of the inquiry was troubling to some who knew his history as a prosecutor. As the *Bulletin* was soon to report, during Wild's ten years as Director of Public Prosecutions he had a history of charging whites with murder but of consistently dealing down Aboriginal killers to manslaughter, or to the lesser dangerous-act-causing-death charge. That was fine, if you viewed the DPP's function as carrying out social repair work. But the effect of Wild's tenure as DPP, in my view, was that Aboriginal victims were treated as less important.

Under Wild's watch, from 1996–97 to 2005–06, twelve indigenous people were convicted of murder compared with sixty-two convicted of manslaughter and forty-seven of a dangerous act causing death. In the same period, thirteen non-indigenous people were convicted of murder, eleven of manslaughter and fifteen of a dangerous act causing death.

Perhaps Wild did not like the Territory's mandatory life-sentencing regime, which required a convicted murderer to serve a minimum of twenty years, whereas in other states a (one-victim) murderer could expect to be freed after serving seven to fourteen years. Perhaps Wild looked at the degraded lives of Aborigines, their environment, their hopelessness, and took that into account when offering manslaughter deals to the defence. And perhaps he took into account the reality that running a full-dress murder trial was always difficult with Aborigines, because they tend to clam up in the witness box.

Wild's was a compassionate, pragmatic view, but it wasn't often that you'd hear of a white person – who might fit every definition of "white trash," with poor education and poor opportunity – being dealt down to manslaughter. And what did the Aboriginal communities make of Aboriginal killers returning home after short stints in prison for killing their wives? That black lives were worth less than white lives? Judges and prosecutors often talked about "sending a message" to the community. The message in the case of Aboriginal man Trenton Cunningham was a particularly challenging one. The DPP – not Wild, but his successor, who nevertheless typified the official approach to Aboriginal homicide – dealt Cunningham down to manslaughter, despite the strong case against him. Cunningham got six years and six months for the manslaughter of his wife and the mother of his four children, Jodie Palipuaminni. Cunningham had bashed her on twenty-nine previous occasions. Experts had predicted at an earlier, 2003 court hearing, at which Cunningham was jailed for pouring boiling water over Jodie, that he would one day kill her. And Cunningham did, over a long night of thumping in 2005. Why this was not a murder was anyone's guess.

Down in Alice Springs, Nanette Rogers, the chief Alice Springs prosecutor, was going it alone, refusing to deal down wife-killers to manslaughter, especially if they had a violent history which showed a longstanding intent. They would be treated as murderers, if the case was good enough: no more manslaughter deals with the defence.

Wild had only ever personally prosecuted one Aboriginal child sex abuse case in his time as DPP, and despite overseeing the GJ and Pascoe debacles, was now being pulled in to look at the problems of children.

Wild was a decent bloke in every way but his appointment didn't sit well with me. Same with Pat Anderson, another popular figure in the north. She was a phone-ducker – when the heat was on in some important matter in Aboriginal health, which was her area, Pat never called back. She was great when it came to off-the-record conversational truths, but the question was whether Anderson would have anything tough to say – and, more widely, whether the inquiry would look in the right places. Anyone with any knowledge of the Territory knew that the problem was not child sex abuse but the brutality visited on Aboriginal wives and mothers. That was the emergency – it always had been. With mothers dead, and fathers jailed, children were either farmed out to reluctant relatives who had their own problems or into foster families. This was when children became most exposed to real risk. An inquiry, if it was to be genuine, needed to go straight to the heart of the violence Aboriginal adults committed against each other. It should have been public, not secret; it should have been along the lines of the South African Truth and Reconciliation Commission, involving people from all parts of Northern Territory society. The Anderson–Wild inquiry visited forty-five towns and communities, taking evidence in-camera, trying to build a picture of something it was not certain existed. The result was the *Little Children Are Sacred* report.

Clare Martin had the report in rough form and Mal Brough was becoming fractious, wanting to see it; so were many others, but it was "at the printers." There was speculation, including from Brough, that the Territory government was using the time to edit and soften the report. I wondered about this, too, but all reliable sources had it that the inquiry's authors had sent their lengthy report to the government as a Word document, which needed to be designed, laid-out, edited (for grammar, as distinct from eradicating unpopular recommendations) and printed in book form.

Upon its release, at a Wild–Anderson press conference, we learned child sexual abuse was happening in "almost every" community. But in all the towns and communities visited, where the board heard evidence, they were sufficiently disturbed to relay to police only six allegations of what they regarded as reportable instances of child sexual abuse. How then was it happening in "every" community? Where was the evidence?

Despite the strong argument circulating around the nation at the time that welfare reform was a key to improving life in communities, *Little Children* did not discuss it. Rather, it employed a warm and meaningless bureaucratic language, with breathless use of bold italicised words and exclamation marks to make its points, such as: "What ... can lead them out of the malaise? Empowerment!"

The authors knew what the real picture was, and even wrote about it, saying in their introductory overview: "[T]he parents of Aboriginal children in many communities are failing to accept and exercise their responsibilities. The word, abuse, in communities, in relation to children, may be given its wider meaning of neglect in social work terms. The literature convinces us that neglect leads to physical and emotional abuse and then, as we have said, in worst-case scenarios, to sexual abuse." That passage nailed the very heart of the problem in communities, though it was the only criticism *Little Children* dared level at Aborigines. In those three sentences was everything they needed to work with and around. But none of *Little Children*'s ninety-seven recommendations sought to address the issue of more general child neglect, which might lead to child sex abuse. The emergency was that children were not being put to bed by 10 p.m.; they were not being properly fed; they weren't being watched and they weren't going to school. If children were cared for, and watched over, in ordinary ways, the chances of them being exposed to sexual abuse would dramatically reduce. Aboriginal parents were always saying: "We can't control our kids, they won't listen," but there was a strong element of cop-out in that. It was the parents who hadn't been listening to the needs of their kids, from the time they could first walk.

I half-expected Territory Aborigines to react badly to *Little Children*. The 'almost every" remark did not correspond with anything in the report and represented the first set of unfounded allegations in the case against

Aborigines. But it seemed no one really read the report; people just took in the general thrust, which was: "Send in the counsellors." So when, immediately after its release, Brough was saying, "Send in the army," *Little Children* naturally became the preferred model.

Brough couldn't quite believe *Little Children*. Didn't they realise toughness was needed? It also left him in a spot. He had expected at least some of his ideas would get a look in – such as ending welfare, ending the permit system and leasing townships to the government. These were his "pathways," but none had cracked a mention in *Little Children*. There was not even an attempt to offer a counter-argument, such as: "Welfare is working" or "Permits are good." There was only one recommendation Brough was interested in, and it was No. 1: "That child sexual abuse in the Northern Territory be designated as an issue of urgent national significance by both Australian and Northern Territory governments."

Martin, having made *Little Children* public, and having known its contents for a month, stupidly said she would not be making any comment on it for some weeks to come. This was all Brough needed. It took just six days from the release of *Little Children* for Brough to override it completely and announce his intervention.

No one knew it was coming. Clare Martin had believed she would get warning of any drastic federal plan because her adviser, Tyrrell, was close to the secretary of the department of prime minister and cabinet, Peter Shergold. But Shergold, busy formulating the intervention, was telling Tyrrell nothing. Tyrrell was by no means incompetent. He understood the politics, fine-detail finances and ramifications of Timor Gap, cross-Territory pipelines and the railroad better than anyone. But he was no good on Aborigines. He'd completely failed to take advice or read the signs on indigenous policy, and had now left his chief minister standing in the spotlight in an open paddock.

Brough and the prime minister's department went into overdrive. It would be in part a mission to transform Howard's reputation as an uncaring, distant leader; in part a shakedown which would see Aboriginal politics changed forever; in part a spiteful assault on Martin. And somewhere among all of this was a notion to protect children from sexual abuse.

It would become clear that the intervention, while drawing from deep ideological springs, was banged together in just a few long days and nights in Canberra. Brough's people would later admit that the policies had no long-term view. That's why they'd called it an emergency. They had run a bulldozer through the scrub. Clear the barriers, they reasoned, and at least you could see what you were looking at. They knew that welfare money was not getting to kids who needed food and clothes; and they knew the permit system stood in the way of any real, if modest, service economies starting up in townships.

Those working around Brough and the cabinet would say the days leading up to the official announcement were the most intense days in politics they'd experienced outside an election. Martin's decision to release the *Little Children* report to the public, but not speak about it, gave Howard and Brough all the authorisation they needed to act. One of Brough's senior staffers told me: "Our concern was they were totally incapable of dealing with *Little Children*. They sat there looking at it, hoping it would change shape. We'd downloaded it off the web, mindful that Martin had said it would be six to eight weeks before she would comment on it. That was the genuinely cathartic moment for us. It was clear they had no plans. You needed a report like this as a call to action. The Commonwealth had the means and will to deal with it directly. We called in the sharpest minds around government. What we then did was take a whole series of pillars, tried to piece them together to respond to the child abuse problem. The time for negotiation was over."

Brough told me *Little Children*'s recommendations were "totally weak and totally inadequate." Howard likewise said he was shocked by the timidness of *Little Children*. "Oh, yes. It was a like barrister making the case and then not calling for a conviction," said Howard. "It was like reports that say, 'We've researched this stuff and we need more research.' I don't think you need more research. For us, one of the fundamentals is the absence of law and order."

The view in federal cabinet was that every single Northern Territory minister was moribund and incapable of guidance or governance. Fuelled by righteous zeal, the PM's department was hammering out its most decisive actions in eleven years. On the day the intervention was announced, 21 June 2007, all I could see was that great things would come of it. I sat on my twig and sang to that tune. A great shake-up had been needed for a long, long time. It didn't matter that Brough could be an insensitive thug. Insensitivity was urgently required. The desire to appear culturally sensitive had neutered every Labor politician who had ever wanted to change the north for the better, just as lack of control in the Senate had silenced every big-talking Liberal minister before Brough.

There was nothing much in *Little Children* that Brough could use to sell his radical reforms to the nation. So he latched on to those two words used by Anderson and Wild in their press conference: "almost every." It would have to do. That, along with the other remark from Anderson, in which she talked of "the rivers of grog." In the days that followed, Brough dropped the word "almost"; it became a fact that child abuse was occurring in "every" community. Brough's claim that he had relied on *Little Children* as his call to arms was only true to this extent: it was what the report hadn't said that most horrified him. Kevin Rudd, opposition leader, was taken aback by the force of the emergency proposals, but stood in the House and quietly stated that he would, without qualification, support every aspect of the intervention.

The emergency-response legislation would be in place for five years and the intervention was to take place in three stages: an initial stabilisation period, which would nominally last a year and seek to establish order through increased police presence, changes to alcohol and pornography laws, the quarantining of welfare, the gathering of population data, and explaining the intervention to residents of seventy-three communities and forty-five town camps; followed by the longer normalisation stage, in which communities would – it was hoped – be provided with the services they needed for good health, education and infrastructure; and the final stage, which was the exit strategy.

Brough decided to involve the army in the early days of the intervention to add a touch of shock-and-awe theatrics. The first community to be "secured" was Mutitjulu, alongside Uluru, which Brough believed was a major nesting site for paedophiles. This was the place where Brough's department had already installed an administrator in the belief that the Aboriginal-run town council was corruptly bleeding money. It would later be found that the administrator's appointment was illegal and that there was no evidence of corruption. The great irony of Brough moving in to "rescue" Mutitjulu was that it was due to his department's appointment of the administrator that the township was no longer functioning. The administrator was mostly off-site, poring over documents looking for evidence of wrongdoing, while the community's vehicles and equipment were under lock and key. Rubbish wasn't being collected; firewood was not being delivered to the elderly. The child-care centre wasn't functioning. The only things operating normally were the primary school and the police station, both run by Brough's nemesis, the Territory government.

Some months earlier, Brough had gone to Mutitjulu to open a brand-new police station and copped an earful from the locals, who were angry that they'd been the target of so much of his disparagement. It was reported that, upon hearing that Mal was coming in with the army in the days after the intervention was announced, women gathered up children and bolted for the sandhills to hide, fearing a new stolen generation. The 7.30 Report's Murray McLaughlin was one of many members of the national press gathered to watch the Mutitjulu takeover, the first physical act of the intervention.

"The stuff about women grabbing children and running to the sandhills was crap," said McLaughlin. "It never happened. What I saw was a bunch of Aboriginal people who wanted answers and didn't get them. Given they'd been the centre of the whole picture, and given that Brough had been given a fair old rumble by them when he opened the police station not long before, they were very polite. There was a bit of tension. The impression I got was they were frustrated. There were a few Norforce blokes sitting around, looking pretty nonchalant, there were some senior army officers, and there were some NT and federal cops, all in uniform. The floor was held by the boss of Family and Community Services, from Alice Springs. There was an air of apprehension, from him. He went out of his way to say they weren't about to steal their children. He was at pains to give that assurance, which reflected the apprehension on the part of these officials at the speed of the whole thing.

"What the people were crying out for was a restoration of normal services. All council plant, vehicles and equipment were locked away, under administration. People were more concerned about getting their resources back and working. The place was on its knees and had been made to suffer, with a lot of ordinary people caught in the crossfire. Given the court case was still running, the urgency of the whole intervention, and the complete ignorance of what it all meant, and that the visiting team wasn't able to answer their questions, the people were remarkably receptive, really." And then most of the intervention crew jumped on a plane and left, leaving a couple of soldiers to kick footballs with the kids.

As this was happening I headed east, into Arnhem Land, to try to gauge the feelings of the people of Maningrida and Ramingining. The people were seeing television images from central Australia of soldiers and police moving in. I encountered Arnhem Landers who were literally watching the roads for the army. I travelled about the place with Wayne Campion, a 53-year-old Maningrida man who was, like everyone else, uncertain what the intervention meant for him. "So, what is the army going to do out here?" he asked me. "Will they have guns?"

"Nah," I told him. "They won't bring guns. They'll just show their faces, lend a hand. It'll be sort of like when they came here after Monica." Cyclone Monica had ripped through Maningrida in April 2006, tearing off roofs and downing huge trees. The place was without power for days. "But the army never came to help us after Monica came through," said Campion. "No one came. Nothing."

National emergencies could be selective things. I wrote:

People we meet along the road are not sure what's going on. Have they lost their land rights? Have we seen military on the road? We pull into Ramingining and find an older man, Matthew Dhulumburrk, watching, waiting. As we talk, a crowd gathers. They're desperate for information.

"I watched Kerry O'Brien question Mal Brough the other night," says Dhulumburrk. "People are panicking. Is John [Howard] coming here for a specific purpose? John and Mal Brough haven't let us know. Why not inform Yolngu people? If John knows there are sick people, child abuse, pornography, ganja, he should have sent his workers here and we could have dealt with it. He didn't believe us. He didn't trust us that we could do things by ourselves."

Dhulumburrk's dead right. John didn't trust them. And with reason. Everyone in this group agrees children in this seemingly tranquil little community wander free at night. School attendance is lousy. "At nights," says George Banbuna, his face heavy with ceremonial paint, "the beds are empty. Kids are walking on the road."

Not much grog is smuggled in here, but these are the kava lands. There is a big red sign just east of Maningrida which denotes the point where kava becomes legal. It's not hard to tell when you've crossed the kava line. You'll begin to notice people with white, scaly skin and road-map eyes.

Kava was introduced to break the grog. It did; but created something else. Kava is drunk ceremonially in Fiji; here, it's drunk all the time. It engenders a soporific malaise. Parents are unable to rouse themselves to prepare kids for school, or themselves for work. Steady drinkers take on a shell-shocked appearance.

Adults can buy six 100-gram bags each week, at $15 a bag. Or they could. Howard and Brough will end commercial kava importation. The Ramingining kava shop – like others in Arnhem Land – will close once the stock has depleted. That's three weeks away. Kava profits have been directed towards community needs, but at high cost. One young man we see is so cursed with "crocodile skin" that he is clearly in pain.

The Ramingining people seem less worried about the closure of the kava shop: they know it's been a rotten influence. But they regard inspecting children for sexual diseases as horrific. They say it should happen to all Australians, if any. And they're horrified about having their community opened to all-comers. The irony is they're suddenly very keen to have the media in to put their position forward.

"Family allowance goes to cards, grog, kava and ganja," says Banbuna. Ramingining people agree, strongly, that welfare payments should be part-cordoned so that money is guaranteed to get to kids for food. At the same time, in that baffling, self-cancelling Aboriginal way, they don't.

"Let's do it ourselves and become people," says Dhulumburrk. "Real people. Let's share our money with our kids." Too late for that. They have, at least for the time being, lost control of their lives.

Whether the PM sees his emergency through till after the election or not, he's rattled them. "Yes, it's a wake-up call," says Dhulumburrk. "A frightening one. Hey, Paul, a bomb is going to land. But where? Is it on my house or on the shop, or where?"

I can't say. Just watch the sky. Or the road. Either way, it's coming.

The Ramingining men had their arms and chests painted in big red circles outlined by white paint for a major ceremony to (as I understood it) invite back the spirits of the dead. It looked like a good photo and I asked if I could take one. They politely said they would prefer if I didn't; it was an "open" ceremony, but they were sensitive about it. No problem. Back in Maningrida, the town was alive at night, not with drunks, but with people attending two initiation ceremonies. These people were likewise not practising culture for the benefit of tourists, but because it meant something to them. It was real, and this was what concerned me most about Howard and Brough's intervention: that the valid parts of their culture might be killed off as the necessary lifestyle clean-up began. I went on (and on):

Maningrida has a 68% school truancy rate. This reflects the slack attitude of parents, and something else: they do not value the western education. Middle-aged men like Peter Danaga, a liaison officer, who was educated and has worked through his adult life, are entitled to wonder. He's no pisshead and doesn't do ganja or kava. He lives in a tiny, rotten, concrete box. He doesn't own a car.

Danaga's youngest son is aged ten. He thinks the boy should learn the Aboriginal way first. "I hope my son will be like me. I'd like him to learn my culture before he becomes a doctor or a lawyer. Yes, he can be both. It's entirely up to him.

"It's true we as parents have to be tougher [and get kids to school]. But we think ceremony is more important than school." Danaga says parents would bundle their kids off to school if they felt some good would come of it. But they can't see the point.

On Friday night, last week, Maningrida leader Ben Pascoe's two-bedroom house gave shelter to sixteen people. There was: Pascoe, his wife, two sons, his wife's mother, her sister and her two sons and daughter, Pascoe's wife's cousin plus her two daughters, another male teenage cousin, and a young man and his two sons.

For dinner they ate local crab and fish, with foreign rice and noodles. Everyone had enough to eat, says Pascoe; they always do. No one regarded the house as crowded. "No," he says, "in the old times, people would feel comfortable camping close in one area. We still do it now."

Outsiders view such close living as the cause of many problems. Indeed, it was in this house that some of the sex crimes against the young boy were alleged to have been committed. Pascoe is an old mate. I've watched him become increasingly resentful of interfering whites; I've seen him dump a good job as a police assistant because of it; I've watched him sit with accused relatives in court, resenting the white system. And, as Aborigines are asked to get with Howard's new program, he is getting angrier.

Brough's department has been advertising for "resilient, highly organised" executive-level staff to come to places like Maningrida for twelve-month stints to take control. They are warned accommodation may be a tent; that spouses and children will not be permitted.

The fear is that a brigade of righteous public servants in long socks and sandals is about to make an even worse mess of everything. A wise old hand on these lands says it will be interesting to watch who'll take up the jobs. "Imagine the kind of tool we're going to get. Imagine how cranky this guy's going to be in November, living in a tent as the wet season sets in, with no piss, no dog, no missus."

Let Howard and Brough do their work. Most of what they propose is right. But they have to take the people with them. To destroy the culture of the north would not be a crime. It would be a sin.

Back in central Australia, where the government deemed the intervention most urgent, Northern Territory and Federal police, joined by a handful of officers deputised from other states, spread out across the communities. And immediately found they had almost nothing to do apart from running the odd roadblock, inspecting for vehicles for alcohol, and generally showing their presence. And, to Mutitjulu's amusement, one of their new Federal Police-officer guardians, a woman, got smashed at the nearby Yulara resort on one of her first nights and was accused of trying to feel up a female Yulara staffer. It was all a misunderstanding, of course. No charges laid.

I met this officer and she did not know that I knew. In truth, she seemed very nice – the perfect cop for this kind of situation: interested, concerned, friendly. She seemed prepared to hang in the breeze and get a sense of the place. I suppose a few places got the worst kind of brick-headed, pin-eyed copper, but I did not meet them. The cops I saw were treading softly, hanging out and talking to people, no guns on their hips. This was not monstering, it was assistance – and many communities had been begging for this kind of presence for years. Away from all the politics, what had begun, in my view, was the most positive period in the history of Territory Aboriginal–police relations.

Last drinks had been called in the remote Northern Territory, but some thirsts you can't control. Meanwhile, in the main towns of the Northern Territory, where the extra police were really needed and the high levels of violence continued unchecked, the bouncers were anticipating a long night.

Until Brough came along, the Labor Left had claimed moral ownership of all matters pertaining to Aborigines, though the NSW Labor Right Aboriginal player Warren Mundine was more concerned that his people were hurting. He helped break the old Labor spell in his stint as ALP president, demanding the party wake up to itself and try a national bipartisan approach. Yet the Left remained desperate for Rudd to savage Brough and Howard over the intervention and was beside itself with frustration when he stayed silent. But not only was the Left failing to offer new ideas, it also needed to show unity and back Rudd in the lead-up to the election.

It was hard to know if Rudd's support for the intervention was an example of the me-too-ism that became such a feature of his election campaign, or whether he genuinely believed the intervention was worth a shot. My guess is that it was a bit of both, leaning more to the latter. Rudd seemed to be a moderniser with no love of ideology for its own sake.

Mal Brough had a coldly realistic feel for remote Australia. When he visited the art centres of desert Australia with the little old bearded women wearing their colourful beanies, sitting around painting dots, he felt no wave of joy; he saw senior citizens toiling while the rest of the population did nothing. He didn't look at an AFL game played between two communities and admire the running and passing skills of boys playing barefoot on gravel ovals; and it wasn't that he came from Queensland, a League state. He'd looked at the players' fifteen-, sixteen-year-old partners, walking through town pushing prams or hip-nursing the next generation of babies, which had arrived way too soon. The result was that these young mothers were taken out of circulation, at such a young age, by the demands of motherhood, in the manner they had for thousands of years. It was no longer appropriate. They had not only lost any chance of higher education, they had lost any chance of completing high school. Who would read their kids bedtime stories? All Brough could see was another incoming lost generation, unable to read or write and, most of all, be employed. He'd sat around listening to the fine words of elders, who were always claiming all problems could be sorted if the kids only had a decent community rec hall in which to occupy themselves. Brough was more or less disgusted. And if a fear-torn shithole like Keats – nice people, bad place – was the best our country could come up with after all these years, he had a point.

Aborigines had always been evaluated against white society. Their culture was never assessed according to its own standards – perhaps because we outsiders never really understood them. This meant that an elder's intimate knowledge of rock-art sites near Oenpelli, for example, was quaint, but ultimately rated as worthless unless it involved a tourism venture. The intimate knowledge anthropologists took from Aboriginal society was available to the few who were dedicated enough to study the work, but it never seemed to filter through to the national consciousness. The odd "bush university" had sprung up in the north, with the aim of impressing upon wealthy or scholarly whites the idea that a deep intellectual reservoir existed. As it did. Similarly, the odd didgeridoo player from north-east Arnhem Land had been labelled a "master" of his art, which he no doubt was; and certain painters had been labelled geniuses, which they almost certainly were. But it was only these people, the masters and the geniuses, who were valued by the outside world, or had any meaningful interaction with it. The majority had been left behind.

Working almost like a journalist, Brough had developed an ear fine-tuned to the rottenness. He'd been collecting anecdote after horrific anecdote which would serve him well on D-Day. Matters pertaining to Aborigines were not easy to sell in the popular press, but the intervention – which the government preferred to call the emergency response – was a national television, radio and newspaper hit. For every policy Mal had a personalised tale of tragedy to back it up. He made it sound real. He didn't talk in general terms – he named places where little old ladies lived behind cages so their sons would not rob them of their pension money;

he knew the trails where the grog and ganja flowed between town and bush. We learned from his tone that every critic of his intervention was an ally of the purported child-rapists. He was an absolutist – there would be no criticism.

What Brough did, first, was to cripple Clare Martin as chief minister. He announced he would seize control of all of the Territory's Aboriginal town land by forcibly acquiring it for five-year periods, and he declared the Northern Territory police force a noble failure by announcing there would be a mass influx of officers seconded from the Australian Federal Police and state police services to stand guard over communities. He would remove the requirement for outsiders to have permits to enter Aboriginal townships (while maintaining the permit system for all Aboriginal land surrounding them). He said he would introduce legislation quarantining 50 per cent of all welfare payments for job-ready people who had been receiving payments for more than two years. He would link parents' welfare payments to their children's school attendance, eradicate X-rated porn in communities, enforce compulsory sexual health checks for Aboriginal children and force people on income support to work to keep towns clean. Alcohol would be banned except at existing prescribed community wet-canteens and there would be no more take-away sales from such clubs. Alcohol was already prohibited on Aboriginal land, but Brough seemed to be saying that the bans would be rigidly enforced.

Called away from her Supercars function to briefings and a press conference, Martin was dazed; her ABC-trained baritone caught a notch higher. Mal Brough had his revenge on her for not deigning to attend his abuse summit the year before. Martin bravely claimed she was prepared to "work with" the federal government, which only confirmed that she didn't get it. She wasn't being asked to work with the federal government – they had just removed her control over governance of half of the Territory. Brough and Howard agreed, straight up, that they'd only done it because it was the Territory. None of the states could be forced to accept interference on such a scale. Martin was also now forced to comment on the *Little Children* report weeks before she had planned to. She could not hide her disappointment in what it had failed to deliver. She'd rightly wanted some firm criticism of Aborigines, as part of a fair apportioning of blame, but there was none of that in *Little Children*. She'd also wanted Canberra attacked, but most of the recommendations had to do with vague notions of education and health and cross-cultural training (for whites, not Aborigines) and seemed to require her spending her own government's money, rather than Canberra's.

In those first days of the intervention, Aborigines and white community CEOs were ringing in, asking me and other journalists: "What's happening?" I'd say: "I'll forward you this press release I just got." But they already had them. Brough's intervention was being conducted by press release. The federal government had no eyes and ears on the ground in the north. It was all alien land to them. They knew Aborigines never thanked Malcolm Fraser for enacting the land-rights legislation which gave them half of the Territory's land; they thanked Gough Whitlam for running sand through the hand of Vincent Lingiari on Wave Hill station. Throughout the years, the Coalition and Labor had, with equal vigour, put the best lawyers onto contesting every land-rights and native-title claim going. It wasn't that either party was anti-land rights; it was that they had a duty on behalf of the rest of the citizens to test every claim to make sure it was valid. But you would have trouble convincing Aborigines that Labor had fought them hard on land at every turn.

Brough couldn't talk to whites in communities because he automatically suspected that anyone who would bother to work in such places was either a lefty or a crook. He found it easy to talk to Aboriginal women, and they to him, because Brough listened, put an arm around a shoulder, and promised he would bring respite from rampaging teenage boys and drunken, raping husbands. He seemed to view all Aboriginal men as potential offenders. He would later tell me: "The sad part is, sometimes you sit in these meetings and talk to people about drugs and child abuse and you know full well that some of the people sitting across the table from you are committing it. They'll say whatever it is you want to hear."

The Northern Territory's two longest-serving federal Labor politicians, Warren Snowdon and Senator Trish Crossin, never personalised Aboriginal abuse by talking about individual cases. They never even discussed rape or homicide or the woeful neglect of Aboriginal kids in broader terms. To do so would, they imagined, aggravate the bush people they relied on to elect them. Both had much to answer for the woeful paucity of debate surrounding the state of Aboriginal life in the Northern Territory; they had hung onto intractable circa-1976 views on Aboriginal land and the people who lived on it. Crossin and Snowdon – "antediluvian," was commentator Nicolas Rothwell's word for Snowdon – both appeared concerned and interested when you spoke to them on a one-on-one basis. But you always had the sense with these seasoned operators that politics, not people, would always take primacy. And they, in their turn, would probably say people like me were naive and didn't understand the political process. And they were probably right. But it didn't mean that one day, somehow, Aboriginal Australians would arise as one from the bush, refreshed and recovered and teeth sparkling, all thanks to Labor.

If there was one Territory Labor figure who had the political experience and cunning to know when a political catastrophe was impending, it was the man Martin once considered her mentor, the retired senator Bob Collins. But Collins had gone up on paedophilia charges in 2004 – mostly involving Aboriginal boys – and was no longer any use to Martin. Bob had done a whole lot of damage thanks to his concealed, violent sexuality. In his way, he'd given some personal sexual violence training to some of the remote-area children who would turn up in courts as adults.

What it meant for Martin was that friends were hard to find.

THE SKI BEACH CON AND OTHER MATTERS

On 4 August 2007, days before Brough was to introduce his emergency-response bills to parliament, the annual Garma Festival cultural picnic was underway in north-east Arnhem Land. Local resident Galarrwuy Yunupingu spoke out against the intervention, saying it was "worrying and sickening, the lowest level of anybody's form of policy." Though no longer holding a position of power, Yunupingu, the old land-rights warrior, remained the best-known clan leader in the nation. Brough didn't regard Yunupingu's comments as helpful to his cause.

Noel Pearson had just completed a deal with Brough for welfare reform in Cape York, and he urged Yunupingu to speak in favour of the intervention for the sake of Aboriginal children. The government badly wanted Yunupingu's support because they believed it could be a potent pre-election statement. Yunupingu was not the kind of man to do something for nothing.

Yunupingu was visited first by Pearson, then Brough and then Peter Shergold, Australia's most senior public servant and Howard's personal emissary. Yunupingu was prepared to listen to Brough and his amanuenses because he had been advised by a trusted ignoramus that the Coalition was going to win the election.

On behalf of his Gumatj clan, Yunupingu negotiated a 99-year lease that would see him sub-lease only parts of his Ski Beach enclave, about ten kilometres from the township of Nhulunbuy, to the Commonwealth. He would retain full control of grave sites, a ceremonial ground and the beach itself, as well as retaining control over an area earmarked for a possible resort. Furthermore, the head lease would be held in Yunupingu's or his clan's name, though he would immediately sub-lease the head lease back to a faceless bureaucrat. There were also published rumours the government had promised Yunupingu an undisclosed amount of money from the Aboriginal Benefits Account – collective Aboriginal money earned from mining royalties – for the resort. There were doubts about the veracity of those reports. In any other circumstances, Brough's view was that if a community was to sign a 99-year lease, and enjoy in return the government's largesse, it had to sign over all town land without exception; but in Yunupingu's case, alone, Brough was prepared to give considerable ground.

Brough presented his signed Memorandum of Understanding with Yunupingu to the nation as a triumph of commonsense and goodwill. It was proof that not only 99-year leases, but the whole thrust of the intervention, could work. It was a con. The deal was no less than a treaty — though not one signed with an Aboriginal nation, but a tiny individual clan within an Aboriginal nation. Such a deal was something the federal government regarded, in all other circumstances, as abhorrent. The deal totally undermined what the government was otherwise trying to achieve with 99-year leases. But all that mattered was that Yunupingu, the only respected tribal leader they could find, appeared to be on side. And Yunupingu duly changed position and began talking up the benefits of intervention.

Some land-rights supporters saw Yunupingu's acquiescence as his final laying down of arms. A condemnatory press statement from the other Aboriginal clan groups in Yunupingu's immediate north-east Arnhem area made clear that they regarded him as a sell-out. Other commentary had it that Yunupingu had been rat-cunning and obtained an excellent deal for himself and his clan.

Yunupingu had, in fact, only signed a memorandum — he hadn't actually got his signature on the final 99-year lease. The document was worthless. And nor had he signed a lease by the time the Coalition lost power. Last heard, Yunupingu had been ringing the office of Labor's Indigenous Affairs Minister, Jenny Macklin, seeking closure on his 99-year lease. Macklin told me she was "talking" to Yunupingu. While she said she was looking at land-tenure issues, she did not seem in any hurry to pursue Brough's 99-year agenda. Macklin had other ideas.

*

An enormous legislative package comprising six acts, headed by the *Northern Territory National Emergency Response Act 2007*, was passed by the House of Representatives on 7 August, with a one-day Senate inquiry on 10 August. The Senate passed it into law on 17 August. Pretty much everything promised, apart from the compulsory sex-health checks of children, which had been uniformly decried as base and offensive, was delivered. Because many of the measures were by necessity racially discriminatory, the legislation needed to be put (the government hoped) beyond legal challenge: provisions of the *Emergency Act* were excluded from the provisions of the *Racial Discrimination Act* and the Territory's *Anti-Discrimination Act*.

No government employee would need a permit to enter Aboriginal land, and no person would need a permit to enter common areas of indigenous communities, as of 18 February 2008. Aboriginal towns would be considered "prescribed land," with most communities, and many town camps, subject to direct Commonwealth control for a period of five years (the life of the *Emergency Act*); Territory and Federal police would have new powers relating to liquor, protective custody and pornography; business managers would be appointed to oversee communities; welfare recipients would be subject to income management; and Brough promised compensation would be paid by the Commonwealth to traditional landowners whose land had become subject to compulsory acquisition (with the exception that seized Territory government assets would not be subject to compensation). The Territory government would be expected to continue supplying services, such as education, health, power and water, as usual.

There were various other changes. The baby bonus would no longer be paid in a lump sum, but in thirteen separate instalments. This was a sensible measure to try to ensure that the money went on the baby, not to a husband who wanted the money for a drinking binge in town. The protective custody powers granted to police meant a person deemed under the influence of drugs or alcohol could be taken into custody even if they were in their own home. Previously, that could only happen if a person was deemed under the influence in a public place. It was an intrusive law, but there was no noticeable outcry from the lawyers. The longstanding reality in Territory towns had been that people would sit at the edge of a community, legally draining cartons of VB, then wander home smashed out of their minds to smash their families.

All Territory residents, white or black, buying $100 or more worth of liquor now had to produce identification, have their name and address recorded and state where they intended to consume the liquor. I looked down one such list. Previous signers had nominated locations such as "The Moon." Liquor outlets would have to retain these documents – which looked no different from a petition you might find on a shop counter – for three years. It was designed to identify potential grog runners to communities. With this mild inconvenience, some of us whites might have got a tiny sense of what it was like for Aborigines, now having their lives so closely monitored – but most white drinkers were telling me they saw it as a grotesque imposition. Personally, I didn't care. It just added a few seconds to the time it took to swipe your credit card, and if they (as some speculated) were really trying to compile a list of the Territory's white pissheads, it was easy to get around: just buy $99 worth of liquor, every day. No one would ever know. I had written, as a joke, that far-flung Aboriginal residents could avoid the liquor controls by joining mail-order fine-wine clubs. Then Tennant Creek police revealed alcohol was finding its way into bush homes via Chrisco mail-order Christmas hampers.

The emergency response also required that sentencing judges pay no heed to customary law or cultural practice that might justify an offence (and while this was directed at Aborigines, presumably all cultures would be affected). This appeared to be in response to Chief Justice Martin's decision to send the Yarralin man, GJ, to prison for a month for viciously sexually assaulting his child bride.

The Territory government felt it had already largely dealt with this issue in one of its own earlier legislative amendments, which prevented barristers from standing at the bar table and explaining to a judge how customary law ("The kadaitcha man made him do it, Your Honour" or "My client believed he had a right to touch his promised wife") had been a factor in an assault. The word of barristers was no longer good enough: they now had to call witnesses – senior Aborigines or anthropologists – if they were going to run the line that an assault had a basis in custom.

This was a sound amendment that closed down those lawyers who purported to speak for Aboriginal law when representing clients. The amendment was accepted by the Territory bar. Still, Territory lawyers were right to object to Brough's new requirement. Their argument was: if people on Aboriginal communities lived pursuant to a system of lore, and there were still many traditional communities that did, then that governed the way they saw the world and the courts should be able to consider a person's actions in the context of the environment in which they lived.

If evidence could show a person's actions were significantly affected by their environment, it could mitigate the level of criminality, and therefore the amount of punishment imposed. None of which meant a man could have sex with his child bride under any circumstance. In 2002, Clare Martin had ended all that with a legislative amendment making sixteen the age of consent for girls – all girls. Aboriginal men were no longer permitted to take or rape promised child brides. It cost her her friendship with Galarrwuy Yunupingu, who said Martin was unravelling his culture.

What Brough's amendment meant was that if, for example, a council of Aboriginal elders prescribed the non-fatal payback spearing of a culprit, and the culprit (as had happened) consented to this punishment, a judge could not take Aboriginal payback law into account in a way that might reduce the man's white-law sentence.

But, as has already been shown, it was white judges who needed to be held accountable, not black law. In the GJ case, Justice Martin had stuffed up, badly. He'd put GJ's belief in his customary rights ahead of the girl's ordeal: he'd given a sentence that was far too low. It was corrected on appeal. In introducing his law, Brough was just throwing his weight around.

Closing towns and the roads leading to them was the great mistake of Malcolm Fraser's legislators when they drafted the *Aboriginal Land Rights Act 1976*. They were right to ensure that the greater part of claimed land could not be trampled over by outsiders; otherwise the rights would have been meaningless. But that outsiders would need permits to visit the towns, built with public money, the places of schooling, policing, the clinics and stores – this requirement made possible most of the degradation and chaos that arose in these communities. People came to live in filth, away from all scrutiny. On visits to communities you would be asked not to photograph the houses or the humpies on the outskirts. People were embarrassed by how they lived. Over the decades, a succession of slimy whites had taken control of many Aboriginal town councils. And it seemed they were never training up Aborigines to take over their jobs.

The Territory government had been trying hard to unearth corruption by white gatekeepers in the Aboriginal town councils and had some dedicated investigators on the case. There was a strong will to expose and prosecute, but the problem was always the same: mangling – or not recording – minutes and inadequate record-keeping worked in the favour of the investigated, not the investigators.

In an Aboriginal community, "expenses" came to mean anything at all: a white town clerk could take his four best Aboriginal mates, put them up for three nights in a Katherine hotel, feed them food and liquor, claim it as a cultural necessity, and then the whole bunch would return home fat, fucked and happy. The modus operandi was to form allegiances with a handful of powerful male leaders who controlled who came in. Journalists were bad news and generally not welcome; tourists rarely visited, and across the Territory there was only a handful of businesses such as eco-camps or fishing lodges which might have brought non-government money in. The interaction with the outside world was minimal and it was not hard to find women, particularly, who were living in fear of small cliques of black and white bullies. To encounter such people, to hear them beg you not to name them lest they be attacked once you were gone, was heartbreaking.

The permit system was insidious in that it also worked in reverse – it kept people in. Many young Port Keats men could claim to have done time in Darwin's Berrimah Prison, but no Keats man – and they were distinctive for their tall, lean, powerful physiques and take-no-prisoners attitude – had played in the Northern Territory Football League in two decades. No artist from Keats had had work displayed in the Northern Territory Aboriginal art collection of the Darwin Museum. It was as though this, one of the biggest communities in the Territory, was an anti-Shangri La protected from the world by a big river, the Daly, and a poorly maintained dirt road. Yet it was only a short light-plane flight from Darwin.

Talking to young Keats men was hard going: most couldn't speak half-decent English (the girls seemed better educated in the basics). When mandatory sentencing was at its peak, there was to be a mass-sentencing of Keats men in the local court. It was not possible to get a permit to report on proceedings. The thinking in Keats was they didn't want their town's reputation further damaged. The law meant not just Aborigines but police, nurses and teachers escaped public scrutiny. People have said I have something personal against the permit system because I was prose-cuted for breaching it. The facts of this particular case are worth recount-ing because they show my presence in Port Keats was not, originally, designed to challenge permits but to monitor Northern Territory police.

Police at Keats had for years been organising public fist-fights as a way of dealing with clan-based gang warfare. It wasn't like a police boys club, where kids boxed under a ringmaster's supervision. Young men were selected and ordered to fight for the reputation of their clan.

At one such supposedly controlled riot in 2002, a young man, Tobias Worumbu, appeared in the crowd with a single-shot shotgun and fired it into the ground. A boy from the opposing gang, Robert Jongmin, attempt-ed to disarm Tobias by tackling and wrestling him. The acting police ser-geant, Robert Whittington, pulled out his Glock pistol and started firing.

Worumbu was hit in the elbow and Jongmin through the back of his neck. Jongmin died. It was atrocious police work. Whittington's bullets slammed into a nearby occupied house.

When it came to the boy's funeral, the police turned up in the Darwin Magistrates Court and advised the magistrate, who was planning to attend her normal Keats circuit hearing the next week, to cancel. They said they could not guarantee her safety, because hundreds were expected for the funeral and police expected it would turn violent. She duly cancelled her circuit hearing. I learned that Territory rapid-response police, armed with shotguns, were to be sent to Port Keats to watch over the funeral. Because one of their members had shot and killed a young man, I took the view that police might again take armed action against Aborigines. I was working for the *Australian*, it was an important Australian story, and I wanted to be there. The white gatekeeper denied me a permit, so I went anyway and was arrested and charged.

Instead of running a free-press case, I pleaded guilty at the first opportunity. The magistrate decided not to convict or fine me. The supposedly independent Director of Public Prosecutions, acting, one suspected, under pressure from the Territory government, or perhaps the land councils, appealed. The prosecution had presented my crime, of entering a Territory town, as high-end criminality, up there with the burglars and rapists. The presiding Supreme Court judge was David Angel. In 2002 I'd watched him give a young Aboriginal man a fully suspended sentence for burning a shed to the ground and severely clubbing various family members (including his dad, who lost an eye, and two small children) with an iron bar because Angel accepted an argument that a kadaitcha man had instructed him to do it. The explanation was probably less ethereal: the young man was wildly drunk when he attacked his family. I had the heavy feeling that for entering Aboriginal land without a permit there would be a price to pay in Angel's court. And so there was: no fine, but a conviction, the worst thing you could do to a journalist, so often required to declare a criminal conviction on travel documents. The full bench of the NT Criminal Court saw reason and overruled Angel, reinstating the magistrate's original decision: no conviction. For its time-wasting, Rex Wild's Office of Public Prosecutions was ordered to pay costs.

During my case and its appeals, it was clear that my own kind, journalists, were in favour of the permit system as well. There was a clear sense that entering Aboriginal land was a nasty, disrespectful business, and that maybe I was a redneck. But some of my colleagues didn't seem to have necks at all – certainly not ones they'd put on the line. Most Territory journalists seemed to think like Angel – one even asked when I was going to apologise. In time, journalists slowly came to the view that perhaps they should not require a permit to report what happened in public courtrooms in otherwise closed towns.

In 2005, a joint letter from most Territory media was written to the NT attorney-general, Peter Toyne, requesting the legislation be changed to allow journalistic access for court cases. Many months later, a letter finally came back from the new attorney-general, Syd Stirling, the member for Nhulunbuy: get a permit if you want to report court cases in Aboriginal communities. Syd was a good guy – with a north-east Arnhem Land electorate that was 90 per cent Aboriginal. He wasn't going to rock their world. But he was attorney-general, which presumably meant he held views that went beyond his immediate electoral position. The gutlessness was astounding.

Discussion of the permit system had begun and it rapidly moved beyond the question of court access and on to the value of the permit system itself. In 2006, Brough released a discussion paper on permits and began calling for submissions. Neither he nor anyone else was suggesting the permit system be abolished altogether. The review related strictly to townships.

The Media Entertainment & Arts Alliance decided to make a contribution, arguing that towns should remain closed. While purporting to represent journalists, they never once bothered to ring a Territory-based journalist to seek their opinion on the permit system. When the MEAA submission became public, I wrote in the Bulletin on 21 March 2007:

The Media, Entertainment & Arts Alliance is supposed to represent journalists. Instead, in a submission to the federal government on whether the permit system should be overturned so that journalists can gain full-time access to Aboriginal communities, it has taken a paternalistic and limited view, supporting the continued closure of communities to media scrutiny.

Most disturbingly, the MEAA has presumed to act as a mouthpiece for Aborigines, arguing that it is overcrowding, poor health outcomes and poor policing levels that need to be addressed, not the permit system.

We already know that about the problems in communities. But we would know a whole lot more if we were allowed to visit them.

Just before Christmas, three petrol sniffers at Gunbalanya, or Oenpelli, in western Arnhem Land, became trapped in a shipping container and were overcome by fumes. Two died. No journalist was allowed near the place, despite repeated efforts by some to get there.

Did we want to drool over their corpses? Did we want to point the finger of blame at the people of Gunbalanya? No. We wanted to tell a sad story and remind people – despite some recent claims to the contrary – that petrol sniffing is anything but a thing of the past. It is real, it continues. The effect of the media ban was that this important story attracted no more than a few lines in the press, and a few seconds of television using file footage of the community.

The MEAA submission is full of statistics and seems to rely on one or two very shrill pro-permit voices to dismiss the concern of most journalists. It also plays favourites by naming a few "preferred" journalists, contemptuously dismissing the majority it is supposed to represent. It points out that two journalists from the *Australian* won a Walkley last year for their coverage of indigenous affairs. And this is the frustratingly stupid thing: that story was centred on the fast-art warehouses of Alice Springs, where people are encouraged to produce shabby art for dealers. No permits are required to report in Alice Springs. [...]

The media used to be called the Fourth Estate, suggesting that within it resided one of the principal tenets of democracy, along with government, judiciary and church. It's not called the Fourth Estate much any more, but it still plays just as important a role (and, indeed, has overtaken the church). It is baffling that the organisation that is supposed to speak for journalists does not seem to recognise this, and worse, supports the denial of access to journalists.

It is correct that the media doesn't "fix" things or make them right. All it does is shine a light, and when that light is shone huge change can come about. The most depressing thing about the MEAA submission is that it doesn't seem aware of the culture of fear, and the culture of gatekeeping, which prevents Aboriginal women, particularly, from having a voice. They cannot just talk to the media.

The media are watched when they enter a community; they are hovered over. People who want to tell the truth lose courage and clam up. Talk to them over the phone and they don't want to be named for fear that some white town clerk will come and wag a finger at them for daring to speak, or be rounded on by bullies from among their own people.

It was not just women who were frightened to speak. Earlier in 2007, I spoke to Ambrose Jongmin, father of the boy, Robert, who'd been shot dead by acting sergeant Robert Whittington. Whittington had been charged with committing a dangerous act causing death but, due to a technicality – the *Police Administration Act* required a police officer to be charged within two months of an offence being committed, and Whittington had not been – he walked from court and would face no further action.

From the time of his son's shooting, Ambrose Jongmin had been strongly advised – whether by police, gatekeepers, lawyers, or all, I don't know – that the press, and particularly me, were his enemy. Now, almost five years on, it had sunk in that the reason for my original visit to Keats was not to trample over Aboriginal culture, or interfere in his son's burial, but to observe police. He was furious that Whittington had walked and now expressed regret – he actually said "sorry" – that I had ever been prosecuted. But Jongmin, like many Aborigines, still seemed to believe talking to a journalist was somehow unlawful. He said: "I want to talk to you. Am I allowed to?" I said to him: "Ambrose, you're a middle-aged man. You live in Australia. You don't work for the government. You can talk to whoever you want."

And Jongmin began to talk, finally, slowly, sadly, saying the law had failed him and his son. "It's stuffed up. It's upset the family, it's upset me really bad. How am I going to get on with my life? I don't think there's been justice done there. Really, I wanted to see real justice done by the law, but nothing has been done. What they done there they dropped all them charges and let him out free. My son never pointed a gun at a policeman. He had no gun. He was just there wrestling that boy. My son didn't have the gun. He did not. He was trying to disarm the boy, that's all he was doing. And yet he was shot and died, defending his friends. When that boy ran out with his gun and fired a shot, my son was worried someone else would get hurt. And yet he was shot in the back. I've been trying hard to see him [Whittington] charged for what he done. Like if I went out and shot somebody, I'll be charged with that, I'll be in prison. But because he was a police officer … I don't know." Jongmin said his son had "no children, he was young, didn't have any problem with police, didn't have trouble going in and out of jail and he was eighteen when he shot. Not once he's been in Berrimah, not once. It's all right for the police officer to get on with his life, but I'm going to drag along. I'm not happy. Justice hasn't been done."

It was the permit system that killed Ambrose's son. The idea of police authorising gladiatorial brawls in a public town, and then firing weapons to regain the control they had lost, would have been unthinkable; but out there, where no one needed to know, it was acceptable. When cops were acting unlawfully, what hope did a distressed parent have?

The case, at its depths, revealed the deep attachment urban whites had to the *Land Rights Act*, which bestowed the permit system. Anyone could see that if Aborigines needed cultural privacy they only had to step out of their town's boundaries, where no one could pry or interfere. But to Aborigines and the left-minded people of Alice Springs and Darwin, and even in the southern capitals, changing the Act was not something ever to consider or evaluate; it was one of the Northern Commandments. Supporting the permit system was the essential marker of a white person's position on Aboriginal politics; for Aborigines, it meant the world need never ask some questions of them.

It didn't matter that these fishbowl townships were festering in their isolation. White supporters didn't want to know. Nor did it matter that Brough was not proposing opening up the wider Aboriginal lands – just the towns and the roads leading to them. On permits, Brough was making long-overdue sense.

On quarantining welfare, to be known as income management, you could see what he was getting at, but the implementation was messy. The government believed, rightly, that not enough hand-out money was being spent on food or clothing but plenty was going on grog, ganja and onto the gambling blanket. Most Aborigines got their money in one of two ways – the dole, or the longstanding Community Development Employment Program. CDEP required people to work, usually in basic-skill jobs such as lawn-mowing or office or store work, but sometimes on more specialised ranger or land-care projects. CDEP paid "top-up" money if people worked longer hours. CDEP was open to corruption, with white administrators easily able to fiddle the books to say some favoured person had put in their hours when they had not – but it was the best thing going. It also allowed workers genuine flexibility if they were called away for ceremonial business. In these places, where people died young, there was always a funeral ceremony which people were obliged to attend. Though an imperfect model, which required attention, its wholesale abolition was thoughtless.

When Brough announced that welfare money would be subject to quar-antine, with 50 per cent held in trust by the government and only available to be spent in nominated stores on essentials such as food or clothing, he thought that included CDEP payments. About a month after the interven-tion was announced, the government realised CDEP was not a welfare pay-ment – it was wages. This lent support to the claims of Brough's people that the intervention really had been shuffled together in a few mad days. Had they more time, the drafters of the legislation would surely have real-ised they had no power to quarantine or manage a person's wages.

By October 2007, after the national emergency-response bills became law, CDEP began to be shut down in the Territory (CDEP was not a crea-ture of legislation but of administration – no law needed to be changed to get rid of it). Everyone would now go onto Work for the Dole or straight welfare, a Commonwealth benefit which could be quarantined under the *Social Security Act*. Brough confessed to the CDEP oversight – just as he would quickly admit that his offensive plan to forcibly inspect all Aboriginal children for sexual diseases was more likely to be a form of assault than anything else.

There was ideology behind Brough's decision to do away with CDEP. The management of these programs went out to annual tender, with local white-run community organisations usually winning the contracts and paying the wages, and earning an administration fee along the way. Brough wanted to break them. *Land Rights News* gave an example of how that decision hurt. The Tjuwanpa Rangers of Hermannsburg, who'd been rec-ognised for their efforts at a recent Landcare Awards ceremony, were left feeling humiliated when their CDEP was abolished on 26 October 2007. They'd considered themselves workers, the same as any urban council worker. "This group, which once worked, are now on Work for the Dole," said the Central Land Council director, David Ross. "They are embarrassed and humiliated. They have to register with Centrelink, register with a Job Network Provider, have their hours restricted and have their hard-earned income reduced and quarantined." What the government did in closing

CDEP in the Territory was extraordinary: they shifted some 7000 CDEP workers onto welfare. Hardly in keeping with Coalition ideology.

Brough was frustrated with the slavish adherence to process that seemed to stifle any forward movement in Aboriginal Australia. He was an action man. At Port Keats he demanded people clean and paint their houses. One young man was given paint and brushes and set to work on his own home. He then did his neighbours' and started moving from house to house, because he felt useful. A Brough adviser reported: "So what did they do? They put him in an apprenticeship program. They shouldn't have done that – they should have just got him an ABN and got him to charge handyman rates. The problem with programs and bureaucracies and CDEP is they think about process and not the outcome. It shows the disincentive; people think about programs, not outcomes for individuals."

It was a good call – and a good example of how bureaucracy could stifle individuality. But if the federal government was going to micro-manage the affairs of Aborigines, why couldn't it sort out the hard cases and manage their income on a person-by-person basis? It already did this with certain trashed-out individuals in the cities. But that would have been too hard, and would have undermined the government's shock tactics. Instead, it would be one-size-fits-all.

The government began reinstating full welfare coverage while demanding people prepare to move towards full-time work. It made no sense. Many bush-raised people would never find real jobs, even at the nearby mine-site. How could a person be employed if they couldn't read the safety signs? Even if they packed up their bags and moved to a major town, it would take years before they were truly job-ready. The debate took a subtle turn. What was Brough's real agenda? Did he want to shut down remote communities entirely? Brough's view was that if a town had no self-sustainability, then it had no reason to exist. His people insisted that it was never their plan to shut down the communities ... but if people gained skills and education, they would eventually decide to abandon the bush, and the government would welcome such decisions. Migration to regional towns and cities was already underway, though not in a thought-out manner: people were relocating from the bush to the hovel-camps of Alice Springs, Tennant Creek and Katherine.

The government knew it had to support the bush for the time being in order to prevent more and more people from gravitating to slum life in bigger towns, and town camps from becoming more hellish than they already were. But bush people, not properly understanding the intervention, had started moving to towns anyway. Again, it showed there really was no plan at the heart of the emergency response. The legislation would be in place for five years. The Coalition would watch it over that time, if it held government, and assess whether or not it was working.

Several previously little-known urban Aboriginal women tried to step into the northern Aboriginal leadership vacuum, presenting themselves as spokespeople for bush people, sharply criticising the intervention on behalf of their bush sisters. One such woman, not elected to any position, claimed on an ABC national television forum that she spoke for seventy communities … or was it ninety? Darwin people, black or white, gagged. As for the bush, they had no clue who this person was: but presumably she thought she was on safe ground.

As did a better-known and more credible Territory Aboriginal parliamentarian, Marion Scrymgour, who in late October 2007 gave a heated speech at Sydney University calling the intervention "the black kids' *Tampa*" (by then an old line) and "vicious new McCarthyism" (a new one which attracted more attention, though as a metaphor it didn't really scan). Scrymgour's speech had been read and approved by her boss, Clare Martin, and left Martin's claims that she was prepared to work with the intervention hollow. Another Territory Labor backbencher, Alison Anderson, a multi-language speaker from Papunya, in central Australia, struck back at Scrymgour and other self-fashioned anti-intervention spokespeople with some punishing, well-chosen words to the *Australian*. "It is a disgrace that people who know nothing about living among the poverty and abuse in remote communities have condemned the intervention," she said. "My people need real protection, not motherhood statements from urbanised saviours. I live my law and culture and I will represent my people regardless of what's fashionable. My people need the help and want the help from this intervention."

The residents of four small central Australian communities were the first to have their income managed. There were initially mixed messages, and anger, as a handful of welfare recipients missed out on money during the changeover. Yet some of those who were living under the first effects of the intervention – health checks, increased police presence and income management – were reporting benefits. A group of Aboriginal women from Hermannsburg, in the centre, backed up Anderson, saying intervention critics had no understanding of what it was like to live in the upheaval of a community. No anti-intervention politician or lawyer or alleged Aboriginal spokesperson had an answer to that.

People could choose to have half of their welfare quarantined to their local store, which electronically managed the money for food or essentials (but not cigarettes). Alternatively, if a person wished to spend on essentials in, say, Alice Springs, they could get a Centrelink card which worked at Woollies or Kmart, but not at the bottle shop. The other half of the payment remained available to be used at the recipient's discretion.

The *Australian*'s Simon Kearney, who had followed the implementation of the intervention more closely than any other journalist, said: "For me the seminal moment of the intervention was when those Ntaria [Hermannsburg] senior women, Helen Kantawarra, Mavis Malbunka, Mildred Inkamala, put out a statement supporting Alison. They started standing up for themselves. After that, there was a grog rally in mid-November in Alice Springs and Peggy Brown, from Yuendumu and Mt Theo [the successful Aboriginal-run petrol-sniffing program], got up and spoke. The translation I got was, 'All the half-caste women who are always asking us to support them, where are they today?'

"The other thing, as far as major moments for me, was when I started getting feedback about income management. I didn't really see the point of it until women started talking about being able to sleep through the night, and shops started reporting food sales going through the roof. I realised it was making a huge difference to families and women and children. Mildred said to me that the people who oppose income management are the drinkers." Men had lost half of their liquor money. If that meant the women were safer, and less likely to be assaulted, it followed that the children were safer too.

In his November 2007 concession speech Howard singled out Brough as someone he especially felt for. Howard had realised, too late, what passion was all about. Same for Clare Martin. Two days after Rudd's victory, Martin announced she would stand down as chief minister. She said she was going of her own accord, but it was a half-truth – she had been informed by her party the day before that there was to be a spill motion. That involved a total clearing of the decks, with every position declared vacant for the vote period. Rather than face the vote, Martin resigned. She claimed she was going in order to give her successor, Paul Henderson, plenty of time to prepare for the 2009 Territory election. However, when the subject of the intervention came up she broke down, admitting the last six months had been the toughest of her career. Paul Tyrrell exited in her wake.

The new federal government had gone to the election saying it was unhappy with the way CDEP had been abolished in the Territory. This was no surprise, given that the Coalition had given no thought to what might replace it. Jenny Macklin, immediately upon becoming the new Indigenous Affairs minister, put a moratorium on any further dismantling of CDEP and said she would look at reforming it instead. It did not occur to me at the time – or, from what I saw, to any other commentator – how significant her planned reinstatement of CDEP would be to the whole thrust of the intervention, though this would become clear soon enough.

Labor also indicated they would reinstate the permit system, proving there was still room for pointless idealism in the new Labor mansion. But they would keep one aspect of the Coalition's permit changes alive: government employees could enter Aboriginal townships at any time, and journalists would not need permits either.

On the reinstatement of the permit system generally, Nicolas Rothwell wrote in late January: "It's back to the future: back to an apartheid world, where visitors to the seventy-three main towns and communities of the Territory's remote north and centre can go nowhere without the stamped approval of a Land Council commissar." Rothwell said permits "acted as a coded signal to outsiders, saying: 'Leave your usual assumptions behind on entry, because things are different in remote Aboriginal Australia, educational standards are lower, social capital is lower, housing is worse, food is poorer – but that's all okay, because it's another kind of society.'"

That last phrase was arresting. Certainly, I had made many trips to Indonesia for that very reason – precisely because it was "another kind of society," which offered different visual and olfactory intrigue and imaginings, many of them involving poor people. I didn't exult in their poverty; but I'd confess to holidaying in it. If there were no other kinds of society, I guess you'd never need to leave home, ever.

I knew some middle-income white Australians who liked to go to Indonesia and spend their cash building wells or buying tractors for small villages because it was another kind of society and it made them feel useful. I'd also encountered a white paedophile who liked to spend money on Indonesian children, because it was another kind of society. It was sick, but I couldn't arrest the prick. Any mature society knew it had to take the good with the bad; otherwise it would just shut itself down to outsiders.

But Labor would renew this damaging contract with Aboriginal Australia and ensure there would be no outside engagement, no free-flowing interaction, no human reconciliation, no nothing. It would remain another kind of society, one few would ever see, and from which its inhabitants would find it hard to escape. Like Burma. Or Port Keats.

A resident of Darwin's Berrimah Prison recently explained to me that when white paedophiles arrived in the jail they would, inevitably, be bashed by other white inmates, as part of the sorting process which rated rock spiders as the lowest of the low. Yet Aboriginal men who interfered with children were never singled out for assault by their own kind in prison. It was as if it had never happened.

You would never find Aborigines crowding around a bush court trying to punch or spit on an accused as the local cops dragged him to court. You were more likely to get a crowd supporting the accused. This suggested one of two things: they were either tolerant of abusers, or more civilised. Talk about the way Crown prosecutors cut deals with the lawyers of defendants? Aborigines were the best deal-makers going. The concept of payment to relatives for pain and injury received was well understood: money, dogs, tools, blankets, food, whatever was to hand. Sometimes it even involved the controlled letting of blood, with a non-fatal stab or spear wound to the thigh. These people lived in small towns where every-one knew everyone. Aborigines would often talk longingly about the days of their "hard law," but sometimes the need for peace saw them merciful to the point of negligence, especially when it came to a damaged chattel such as a woman bleeding at the end of a long mulga stick.

The gang-rape by nine adults and teenagers of a ten-year-old girl at Aurukun, in northern Queensland, made international news after the *Australian*'s Tony Koch exposed the case in December 2007: the group pleaded guilty, but the judge decided none of the rapists should serve jail time. The prosecutor had described the rapists as "naughty." Though the victim was not of an age to give legal consent, the prosecutor had said she'd wanted it. The proceedings appeared to have been conducted under sharia rather than Australian law. It was a complete failure.

When the Maningrida gang came up for sentencing in the Supreme Court in Darwin only days later, there was no chance they were going to get such a light going-over. All were convicted and all given short periods of imprisonment. The young victim was unlikely ever to return to life in Maningrida, although there were all sorts of promises to the court that he would be welcomed back. Meantime he, having been extricated and supposedly placed under care in Darwin, was running with a bad crew and had allegedly participated in an armed robbery. The sense was that this kid was not going to be okay.

Anthropologists had a theory that Aboriginal children were allowed to become autonomous at a very young age. It was said to be an ancient survival mechanism that in modern times had given rise to high-level disobedience and delinquent sexual behaviour. The theory seemed pretty right to me. You'd also hear, if you stayed around long enough in the north, that Aborigines didn't feel the deaths of their loved ones quite so deeply as non-Aborigines. There was a white view that Aborigines had become desensitised to emotion. Maybe it was the cruel way men treated women, and their seeming lack of remorse in trials. And perhaps it was because when news of a death was received in a community, certain women would start wailing and striking themselves. Like payback, it was formulaic and ritualised, with wailers tasked to wail and others assigned to collect the firewood for the sorry camp and make sure everyone was fed. One white person who'd been working in a central Australian community put it to me this way – and it was not a question: "Why do you think they hit themselves? Do they need to make themselves cry because they don't really feel upset?"

Just because there was organised grief did not mean that the immediate relatives of the deceased did not feel the loss deeply. Anyone who goes to a funeral in a Greek Orthodox church will see the same thing: the arrival of the little old ladies in black, the professional wailers, who may not have had any liking for the deceased but always turn up for the show. Communal grief is a good thing, or so the Greeks and the Aborigines tell me. And the shrieking coffin-bearing Palestinian crowds on news television seem to agree.

Gatjil Djerrkura had once told me that funerals were the bane of his life: they cost money and time. He could not avoid these responsibilities, which might cost weeks of his time, might involve light-plane charters and require the payment of gifts to the family of the bereaved. I'd seen a similar thing in East Timor when a young man's wife's grandmother died. He was weeping, though not for the old woman. He was obliged to buy a water buffalo at the cost of around $US200 for a funeral feast and would be in debt to the boss who loaned him the money for years to come. There seemed implicit in what Djerrkura was saying, and openly in the case of the young Timorese man, a sense that the dead were robbing the living. Maybe if Aborigines lived longer lives this would be less of a problem.

As for whites, we'd overcomplicated our views about Aborigines. If culture was ethnicity, and ethnicity culture, then I viewed Aborigines as just that: ethnic people. That didn't mean "foreign," as Australians had come to think of ethnicity, but that they belonged to a specified racial, linguistic group which certainly had its share of ceremonial unknowns but was really about family. It made them easier to understand. There was no point in taking a view that Aborigines possessed a collective soul that linked them to land and water and spirits and dreams; just as there was no point in imagining that they were all hopeless. You just had to take people one by one, on face value. That made it easier, too.

The Sisters of Charity, Mother Teresa's crowd, working in Tennant Creek, told me that they thought Aborigines were more content than white people knew. The Sisters had come to Australia believing their work would be mainly with Aborigines, but found the real sadness to be the deep loneliness of white people who lived alone in commission houses or in aged-care homes and had no visitors, apart from the Sisters. Aborigines, they said, might have been destitute, and many might have been forever drunk, but they still had a sense of family which gave them meaning and purpose. The way small Aboriginal children would unthinkingly share their food with other children delighted these nuns.

Us plain-white Australians tended to lose any sense of our relatives once they headed into second-cousin territory. But if an Aboriginal girl said she called six or seven women "Mum," then she probably did. The child would know from a young age that she had a clan and a tribe, and hundreds of relatives. If you were Greek-Australian, it was likely you too would treat distant cousins as close cousins. It was all very charming, of course, if you were roasting forequarter goat sections on the spit as Mikis Theodorakis tunes jangled in the background. In Alice Springs, you were more likely to be working your way through four litres of Fruity Gordo on a hot day and coming to the conclusion that your wife was a slut who needed a sharp tree-branch in the head. And where were the kids?

The reliance on extended family still existed in platitude, but vigilance had gone missing in Aboriginal Australia. The first emphasis was always on the notion of relatedness, of kinship, rather than on any notion of safety. People traditionally shared responsibility for one another's children, but that was a responsibility people were no longer taking up. And, like anywhere in the world, people were usually harmed by people they knew.

DINNER IS SERVED

Major-General Dave Chalmers was the operational commander of the emergency response taskforce. He'd been appointed by Brough and Howard but was now working under Jenny Macklin and Kevin Rudd. Chalmers was one of those occasional fully developed, highly competent senior soldiers. He knew how not to confuse the mission with the politics. He was focused only on what he had been tasked with – and that was a lot. It had seemed to me strange at first, and unnecessary, to put a soldier in charge of the running of such a mission. But when you met Chalmers you knew his view was that the government had given him a clear mandate and he would not stray from it. He said he was not so much holding Aborigines accountable, as government.

Chalmers had been national commander of Australian forces working out of Dili from 2001, where his role was to ensure that the United Nations deployed Australian troops appropriately. He had seen to the deployment of the first C-130 Hercules to Banda Aceh less than twenty-four hours after the 2004 tsunami struck, with a surgical and water-purification team. Those huge black water-bladders which suddenly appeared amid the poisonous ruin of Banda Aceh, and which attracted such long queues of desperate people, stopped a second catastrophe of disease. East Timor and the tsunami were genuine emergencies. Did Chalmers consider this to be one? "The government's declared it to be an emergency," he said.

Yes, but did he consider it to be one? "The government's declared it an emergency," he repeated. "Look, I think there's a crisis occurring in the Northern Territory, probably elsewhere, but my experience is in the Northern Territory. It is a crisis which most people, including myself, who live in mainstream Australia, are either happy to ignore or [remain] in ignorance of. It's confronting to see the poverty and social dysfunction that exist in remote communities, the services that people don't have access to and are unable to access. Even basic things like the ability to procure food. Many remote communities just don't have a reliable source of good food at reasonable prices. When that happens, there are knock-on effects into children's health and adult health."

In January, a mate had rung to say he'd been to an Aboriginal rock and dance performance at the Sydney Opera House. Some MC had raised the horror of the intervention and the crowd had howled sympathetically. It was pretty easy to complain from a chair in the Opera House.

Two thousand kilometres away in central Australia, it was seven months since the emergency response had been announced and it was clear that there had been a subtle but total shift in its nature. Initially the intervention had been dressed up as a kick-down-the-doors child-sex emergency, but by January its agents were taking the more realistic approach of trying to turn the communities into sane, liveable places.

Brough's promise to force all Aboriginal children to submit to sexual disease checks had been the first casualty of this. "In fact that was not a practical or possible thing to do," said Chalmers. "Compulsory checks were not legal and it's not that simple to do a half-hour check on a child to detect sexual abuse. That is a specialist's check that needs to be done by experts and takes time. What has been done, the government decided, was a check of general health – weight and height, skin conditions, social history, the sort of check that every child should receive every year."

The taskforce had deployed individual child-health teams across the Territory and an estimated 15–17,000 Territory Aboriginal children were on track to have, for some of them, their first proper medical examination since they were babies. The teams were finding that 60 per cent of children required referrals, half of them to primary health-care, often with serious ear, nose and throat problems; the other half needed basic dental or skin treatment. Twelve children were found to have holes in the heart and were referred to Darwin or Adelaide specialists. This was very valuable work. If the Opera House crowd resented this, they were ill-informed.

Fears that the legislation, which allowed the federal government to control communities for the five-year period, was a disguised land grab were not justified. The real reason for the five-year town annexation was so that the government, which wanted to spend money repairing and rebuilding housing stock, had a legal basis to control the assets until a more permanent form of underlying tenure was worked out. The Liberal government had hoped this would be 99-year leases over towns. The Labor minister, Jenny Macklin, wasn't interested in pursuing this and came up with a proposed 40-year lease system which would see zoned areas within townships subject to lease so that the housing commission could control housing assets.

"Government business managers" were making their presence felt in communities across the Territory. Some were public servants or cops who had taken long-term leave and were earning colossal away-from-home kickbacks. It was inevitable that there'd be a quota of deadshits sent in; and some of these people were regarded with deep suspicion, particularly in communities with successfully functioning corporations. The fear was that these new managers – some with no background working with Aborigines – would stage takeovers. Chalmers said that while there were reserve powers in the legislation to seize organisations, he saw them "as a last resort and I simply haven't used them."

Chalmers was aware of the danger of creating a new wave of white gatekeepers. "Government business managers don't take over communities," he said. "They're not mission managers, they don't replace the CEO and their task isn't to run communities. For mine, the most important role is that they're the permanent face of government in a community. For the most part communities that have government business managers are very, very positive about the manager, and the reason is they've got someone they can hold accountable for government promises. They've got someone who's living in the community who they can talk to any day of the week about what government said it was going to do."

"There are problems with [welfare quarantining and income management] and these are very complex things to introduce," Chalmers said. "When a problem crops up, it aggravates people … but people who often don't have a voice, they know this is making a difference and money is available to be spent on children. Stores where we've introduced income management have had an increased turnover of 20 to 30 per cent. To me, that money that was potentially being spent on gambling or grog is now being spent on food and essentials."

If income management was discriminatory, Mavis Malbunka, sixty-three, the emerging spokesperson for Aboriginal women from Hermannsburg, in the centre, didn't see it that way. By January she had lived with income management for close to six months. "We see the benefits," she said. "There's no money running out. Income management is a great help for Aboriginal people – in Hermannsburg I hear no complaint about income management." She said it was too early to say whether gambling had been stamped out, because there was still cash available in the un-quarantined welfare payment. "But I do know people are buying more food."

Malbunka had witnessed the initial visit by army and medical teams. She said an infrastructure crew was in the area talking about renovations and building improvements but, as a grandmother, what she really wanted from the intervention was practical assistance with disciplining kids. "Old people and family feel there's a threat coming from the children. If we hurt them, they go to police and we are charged. We are not looking to hit kids, but we want support to work with the kids. They're going over us." Her point was valid: how can you help kids, and protect them from harm, if they won't listen? Therein may have been Dave Chalmers' toughest intervention challenge.

The Little Children Are Sacred report contained unsubstantiated allegations which characterised Aboriginal men as a danger to their children, a claim also made many times by Brough. So where were all the child sex victims? Where were Brough's famous paedophile rings?

The Northern Territory police commissioner, Paul White, said that Operation Themis, which operates separately but in conjunction with the emergency taskforce, had received thirty-six reports of abuse. But there were many variables and the reports were not solely about sexual abuse.

"A lot of the cases," said White, "are child abuse, physical, mental, children in need of care and so on. So it's a bit tricky when you are trying to split hairs and say just how many."

The report of South Australia's Mullighan inquiry into sex abuse in the Anangu-Pitjantjara-Yankunytjatjara lands, north of the state, was released in early May and found it "likely" that 14 per cent of the 1000 children living there had been raped or molested. There was again a disturbing similarity to the Little Children report: there was almost no direct evidence to back up the inquiry's claims. This did not mean there was no abuse; the former SA Supreme Court judge Ted Mullighan relied on medical reports for his findings but expressed disappointment that Aboriginal women had been pressured by their men not to give evidence. And this was entirely possible. But without witnesses, you were left with the feeling you were only getting half the story. These APY lands, like Northern Territory Aboriginal land, were closed to outsiders. Mullighan made no recommendation that they should be opened.

What was apparent – and this was something Little Children should have addressed, but failed to – was that general neglect gave rise to more extreme cases of sexual predation. In the settling period since the intervention commenced, there had been acknowledgment of this. "You'll see from the intervention this is a much broader intervention than simply targeting paedophiles," said Chalmers. "This is about targeting what it is that creates an environment that allows sex abuse to occur at a rate that is much larger than the rest of the community. So it is looking at making [sure that] issues of employment, housing, health and education are all addressed so that the next generation of Aboriginal children have some chance of growing up safe, happy and healthy." It took some strangling of the animal, but the truth was emerging: child sex abuse wasn't the real problem.

Chalmers would not comment on Macklin's decision to reinstate the permit system for townships. Macklin was saying the permit system would keep out the paedophiles and the grog and the ganja. This was odd:

weren't the paedophiles supposedly already in the communities? Wasn't that the basis of the emergency response? As for drug and ganja runners, they were not outsiders: they were Aboriginal locals, looking to make some extra money or taking in their own supply.

Journalists would be allowed in without permits, but so what? It wasn't ever about journalists. It was about allowing normality to return – or begin to return – to the bush. It wasn't even about child sex abuse. But if that was the vehicle politicians had used to sell their emergency intervention, you had to see it for what it was: politics. And if you were still sitting around, months into the intervention, experiencing explosive waves of political sympathy and anger on behalf of Aborigines, it was a fair bet you'd never been to the Northern Territory.

The emergency had turned out to be somewhat less invasive than many had feared. The Northern Territory government, initially shocked by the intervention, then humiliated, was seeing the benefits: it knew that over the five-year period would come an enormous injection of Commonwealth funding to the bush.

Then, on a day in late April, Jenny Macklin followed up her pre-election promise and formally announced that CDEP would be reinstated across the Territory. Many northern towns still had their CDEP programs, due to the moratorium Macklin had imposed upon its further abolition upon taking government, but some thirty townships in central Australia had been living under full income management, and no CDEP, for many months. It finally sank in how momentous her decision to give back CDEP to these central towns would be, and how deeply it would affect the whole tenor of the intervention. If income management was perhaps the most fundamental and successful plank of the intervention, with Aboriginal mothers and grandmothers in particular saying it had changed their lives for the better, the reintroduction of CDEP would mean that Aboriginal men, in particular, would choose to wander back onto CDEP. The government could not touch or manage CDEP incomes because they were seen as "real wages." The bottom line was that men would be able to do their few hours' CDEP work each week, and when it came pay time, could spend their whole income on alcohol, if they wished. Macklin was insisting that income management would still exist for welfare recipients, so that mothers – particularly – would still have their income managed to protect their men from stealing the money for beer. But there was a growing suggestion – denied by Macklin – that welfare recipients would soon be able to choose whether they wanted their welfare income managed by the government.

The Western Australian Greens senator, Rachel Siewert, issued a celebratory press release. She got it right – but hadn't thought through the implications when she said that "the re-introduction of the CDEP scheme in prescribed communities in the Northern Territory in June would result in a rush of willing participants who were keen to escape from the prescriptive welfare-quarantining measures and take control of their own money."

Income management had always troubled me in the way it had formalised racism through legislation, but when struck by such thoughts you were always drawn back to the words of those central Australian Aboriginal women who said their lives, and the lives of their children, had changed significantly for the better after they, and their husbands, had their incomes managed. CDEP was always better than Work for the Dole, but it would see the return of the drinker's wage.

What had been won out of whatever was left of the intervention? The Territory and federal governments, which had long neglected Aboriginal communities, now seemed finally to realise that they had a responsibility to improve living conditions in Aboriginal towns. And the intervention had delivered better policing and broad, non-invasive health examinations of some 15,000 children, which had led to referrals for basic but important problems. It was something. It would be difficult to assess for some years to come whether the clampdown would result in more kids going to school. But in surveys, the interventionists had identified several thousand remote-area children who had never spent a day at school.

By January 2008, big signs had gone up around Alice declaring the whole town a dry area. People found drinking in public could have their drinks tipped out and could be charged. This was something the Northern Territory government had been moving towards before the intervention. Now, with the new takeaway sales restrictions and the heavy fines for drinking in town camps, it was going to be hard for drinkers to find anywhere to get smashed, unless it was under a piece of tin. At least that was the idea. In early April, I took a 6 a.m. stroll down the Todd River in Alice Springs. The riverbed was a sea of green cans. It was illegal to drink along the riverbed, but the Aborigines there were playing hide-and-seek with the authorities. They were shadow drinkers. These were not people who started wondering about that gin and tonic around 5 p.m.; they were chronic alcoholics who needed to drink all the time.

The town camps of Alice all now had big signs warning that alcohol and pornography were outlawed (in some cases, town campers had defaced or ripped off that part of the sign that said "pornography"; it appeared they deemed the word offensive). But the camps looked to me like they always had: places of wreckage and misery. Income management meant half of the welfare money went into a bank account and the other half came in the form of a voucher, which could be swiped for food or essentials at any accredited store. Liquor and cigarettes could not be bought with these cards. According to locals I spoke to, the cards – which were not linked to anyone's name – had become highly tradeable. If you had $200 credit on a card, you could sell it for $150 in cash and head straight to the bottle shop.

There were reports of people shifting out of the Territory, in numbers, to places such as Mt Isa and Port Augusta. Katherine was the next town declared a total dry area, and it needed it. But the effect of the ruling was predictable: that town's drinkers were evacuating north to Darwin, which was not to be declared a dry town. From my home, it appeared these refugees were arriving in unprecedented numbers to make their homes in the long grass where they could be left alone to drink.

It became possible to consider the intervention in terms of a spectacular but short-lived life. It was more or less over, ten months after it had begun. Brough's departure had been fatal. If one definition of "conservative" was someone who liked things how they were yesterday, not tomorrow, it was clear now who the real conservatives were.

The bush had always needed attention, but it was in towns where Aborigines fell through the cracks. It was a matter of record that the worst abuses happened in the main towns, where liquor was most readily available. But at some point you had to stop blaming governments and acknowledge they could only do so much. The legislative possibilities for stopping drinking, short of prohibition, had pretty much been tested and failed. Somehow, chronic alcoholism needed to be addressed – by the drinkers themselves. But self-awareness and the desire to repair and change were not the priorities of alcoholics.

The case of a Darwin Aboriginal woman, Sophia Moreen, was an instructive example of what authorities were facing: she was deemed so far gone she wasn't even suitable for an alcohol rehabilitation course. It was akin to the way doctors might say they wouldn't amputate a gangrenous limb until the patient was strong enough to handle the operation.

Sophia was sentenced for grievous harm of her niece, in the Supreme Court on 9 November 2007. A year before, in Darwin's Bagot community, Sophia had attacked her adult niece, Helen James. The two were neighbours, Sophia living at Bagot's House Three and Helen at House Two. They'd been drinking through the day and the session had got messy. Sophia's partner, Clifford Williams, got angry at Sophia and smashed a small stereo which Sophia and Helen jointly owned. Helen demanded money from Sophia in recompense; Sophia refused to pay. By nightfall, both women were very drunk. Sophia struck Helen with a broken crutch. Helen hit back. They were threatening to kill each other.

The judge: "You then boiled some water, put it in a large pannikin, went to the front door of Helen James' unit and called out, 'Helen, look here.' This caused Helen James to turn towards the door. As she did so, you threw the hot water over her. The water made contact with her left arm, chest, neck and the left side of her face ... the burns were particularly severe on the neck, chest and left arm. They eventually required considerable skin grafting. At first, she did not feel any great pain from the burning. You went back inside your own unit."

In reply, Helen James boiled her own jug and went next door to throw it at Sophia but, very drunk, she threw her hot water against a window instead. The police arrived and saw that Helen was beginning to blister, badly; but Helen refused to go to hospital. Both women then locked themselves in their homes, refusing to co-operate with police. By early the next morning Helen was in pain and needed an ambulance. Her injuries were such that she stayed in hospital for almost three weeks.

Sophia was arrested. In that typical guileless Aboriginal way, she made full admissions in a police interview. When asked what she had wanted to happen to Helen, Sophia told police: "Put her in hospital." This is a common aim of Aboriginal assailants. In Alice Springs people are known to say, as a threat: "I'll ICU you." Helen was discharged after requiring grafts to 9 per cent of her body. Two months later, she attacked Sophia with a knife, stabbing her in the stomach and the back, in what the court recognised as "deliberate payback." The wounds were not serious. The court heard the two women had since made amends. Sophia's lawyer told the judge her personal life had been horrific. And so it was.

The judge: "You were born in 1970, the youngest of a family of nine. Your father passed away when you were a small girl and you have little memory of him. You grew up with your family in a community near Mandorah [just across the harbour from Darwin] and ultimately attended Darwin High School up to Year 10. You then returned to the community at age sixteen and commenced drinking alcohol, because that was what your family was doing, and there was not much else to do.

"You have had four children, the first of which was born when you were still only sixteen years of age. One of those children has since passed away. Due to your young age and your then-escalating problem with alcohol, you were unable to care for your children and they were farmed out to different family members. You have never worked since leaving school.

"At quite a young age, you formed a relationship with a fellow drinker by the name of Clifford Williams and moved into Darwin with him. I am told that that relationship has been extremely violent. Over time, your partner has broken both of your legs and one arm, has severed your knee tendons with a knife, has blinded you in the right eye, has knocked out most of your teeth and broken your nose. Your face and head are said to be covered with scars as a result of the numerous occasions on which he has struck you.

"Your counsel informs me that you have been admitted to hospital on so many occasions that your medical records now occupy some five separate volumes of entries. In the last twelve months alone, you have been taken to hospital by ambulance on five occasions due to the violence on the part of your partner. You have stated that you stay with Clifford Williams because 'most of the time he is all right'."

The judge said Sophia was "normalised to being a victim of violence and experiencing violence and chronic alcoholism in your daily life. It is to be noted that your eldest child was killed after he was stabbed during a drunken fight at the age of twenty-one years. This occurred only about three months prior to the incident now before the court and you were still grieving at that time."

Sophia also suffered from diabetes and acute pancreatitis. She had a "recurrent left side pneumothorax as a result of a previous stab wound inflicted by Helen James on you some time ago and various other alcohol-related illnesses." Furthermore, Sophia, a 37-year-old Australian woman, had tuberculosis, a disease normally associated with Third World countries but reasonably common among Top End Aborigines. This woman was seven years younger than me and had gone to the same Darwin school I had attended for a couple of years. Needless to say, that was where the similarities ended. The school ground wasn't a place where bush and urban kids came together. Full-blood students like Sophia didn't mix with other kids – you'd see them disappearing into demountables at the back of the school for their "special" classes.

The judge said it was "perhaps small wonder that, on the day in question, you resorted to violence to resolve the dispute that had arisen between yourself and your niece." He then gave the standard judge's spiel, saying: "Whilst incidents of violence associated with drunkenness are endemic in Aboriginal communities, this court has made it clear on numerous occasions that it cannot and will not condone such conduct and that it has a responsibility to do what it can to protect other persons from acts of violence." But the courts were unable to stem the violence.

At the time of her sentence, Sophia was being held in isolation in hospital because of her TB. She was such a chronic drinker she was deemed unsuitable, if released from isolation, to attend an alcohol rehabilitation program. Nor could another care program take her until her TB was well under control. Sophia Moreen was sentenced to two years and three months, to be suspended after nine months. The condition was that she attend an alcohol program that would take her after her release.

Sophia will be released from jail in August 2008. The effect of the intervention on her life will be two-fold. She will most likely have her income managed, and she will not be able to drink at her home in the Bagot community, which has become a prescribed town camp. My guess is she will not take well to her new world. She will become more desperate than ever.

Mal Brough changed the law so that Aborigines could not use culture as a defence. I think what he really wanted to do was change the law so that a person could not offer Aboriginality as any part of their defence. I don't know whether Sophia's sentence was heavy or light – I guess it was probably about right – but I do know that a person's background ought to be a crucial element in the court's thinking. The judge rightly was no longer allowed to recognise Sophia Moreen's culture when it came to sentencing, and the truth was she no longer even had one. But he could certainly, as he did, recognise that her Aboriginality was a major factor in her offending. She was both victim and assailant, and a mindless, legless traveller in the ruined romanticism of the north. She was a town girl, not a bush girl. Hers was the real story of the Northern Territory.

Sara Dowse

In 1973 I went to work for the late Clyde Cameron, then the minister for labour and immigration. There was no odder couple. I was a single mother, he was an ex-shearer, a committed unionist who had taken on both the right wing of the Australian Workers' Union and the left of the Victorian ALP. His support for the federal intervention in the Victorian executive had resulted in the Whitlam government's election. Cameron was a hero, a man's man, a fighter. I was a women's libber.

It was only a four-month secondment, but it affected me deeply. The reason for my being on his staff was one of those quirks of the time. After heavy lobbying, Labor women got three new planks on the party platform, all concerning his portfolio. They committed the government to introducing equal pay, part-time employment and child-care in the federal public service and to promoting them elsewhere. Cameron needed someone to develop the policy and write speeches for him; I was recommended for the job.

I was given an office in the centre of Canberra and there, a kilometre or so from Parliament House, I began wolfing down every history, every government paper, every ILO projection on the subject of employment that his department and the parliamentary library could supply.

Maybe it was because my reading was so concentrated, maybe because it was more than academic, but the place of work in a person's life never had such an impact on me as it had then. More than any crummy job I'd had, anything I'd learnt at school or university, anything I'd heard at the weekly women's lib meetings or found in any feminist text, the crash course I took in that lonely whitewashed room radicalised me.

There is always a risk in extrapolating from the particular. On the other hand, as the women's movement argued at the time, it is a person's lived experience that determines her politics. But though personal experience can be a good place to begin, it's not necessarily the best place to end.

Anne Manne begins with the election of Kevin Rudd and the new family paradigm that he and his wife Therese Rein projected during the campaign. It's not for another few pages that she writes of her early work experience, but the example she offers is telling. Before starting university she worked on an outback station, ostensibly as a jillaroo, but more "a domestic slave." Long hours cooking, cleaning and child-minding were the rule. Only before daybreak was she allowed to get on a horse and do the things jillaroos are supposed to do, like rounding up cattle for the market. All in all, it was hot, dirty, gruelling, utterly unappreciated, low-paid work and, not surprisingly, she loathed it.

But what conclusions does she draw from this? The recounting of her first paid labour experience follows a section depicting the hollow victories of women on the corporate ladder, and is meant to show, by contrast, what work for far too many of us is like. And, of course, she's right. But work need not be like that, and I still can't help wincing whenever she implies that feminism is to blame for the long hours and increasingly casualised, segmented labour market that characterises our recent economic boom.

Manne is highly critical of what she calls "Get to Work" feminism. And while it's certainly true that the feminist resurgence at the end of last century overlapped with the return of laissez-faire capitalism, it's too big a leap to say that by demanding equality in the workforce feminists have been concerned only for their careers. Nor is it helpful to suggest that the new market ideology, with its emphasis on individual wealth and recognition, has been a matter of choice for feminists.

Though Manne doesn't explicitly say this, she comes awfully close. Drawing parallels with Max Weber's analysis of Protestantism as a driving force for capitalism, she writes: "Upon what tracks have feminist ideas run? The answer is: market tracks!" Her mistake is to equate the power of feminism, which is considerable, with that of the dominant force in our society. Capitalism finds uses for everything – even, it must be noted, for parenthood and love. Nor have feminists been totally naive about the risks of co-option.

At the core of Love & Money lies this basic question: is unfulfilling, exploitative work better than no work at all? It's not a simple question and has no simple answer. Manne herself draws attention to a fundamental division of labour, one that goes beyond the differences between paid and unpaid, yet addresses the phenomenon of what has become known as the "caring" economy. It's an interesting analytical tool that points, however, to a truly intractable problem. The unpaid work that people (mostly women) do forms the caring economy, but there are also paid professions, such as nursing and teaching, which are, essentially, "caring." Medicine, too, is a caring profession, with the significant difference that most of its practitioners have been men. And there's the rub. Practically *anything* men do has been better remunerated, better rewarded in terms of status, than occupations where women have predominated.

We '70s feminists called this "the sexual division of labour." Honoured since by more sophisticated labels, it was what stared us in the face when we were fashioning our policies. Even in those more socially conscious days, it couldn't be undone just by saying it was unfair. We could have shouted from the rooftops that the most important work anyone could do is to nurture children, but it never would be rewarded commensurately so long as it was mostly women who did it. Arguably, this is no less the case today.

Many of Manne's contentions rest on the assumption that money is equitably transferred within families. The work of economist Meredith Edwards showed that this is far from true. There is no reason to suppose that the unpaid work of looking after children and maintaining a household is any more compensated for *within* the home than it is outside it. This is because, again, for the most part it is women who undertake it.

The key factor in all this is that women give birth to children and, almost everywhere, have been primarily responsible for their care. But this responsibility hasn't always been organised as it has been in modern Western societies, nor were women, by dint of it, excluded from significant economic activity. For most of human history the care of children has been a communal endeavour, not the responsibility of an isolated mother in a suburban home. The challenge has been to find a way through this conundrum, and the solution, as we saw it back in the 1970s, was universally available, community-based, educationally integrated, quality child-care. The aim of this was not only to assist individual women in juggling motherhood and employment but to enable, yes even encourage, the growth of a critical mass of working women whose very numbers, ipso facto, would change the nature of paid labour; to make it, in other words, more "caring." It was a policy designed to help women, men and their children, but it was not a magic wand and, as Noam Chomsky once wrote, "There is no such thing as a riskless policy."

By now we all know how Australia's children's services program, once the best in the developed world, was systematically dismantled by the small-government, private-enterprise ethos through which successive federal governments extended their subsidy to commercial operators. The resulting cost of child-care today, the high staff-to-infant ratios and generally lowered service are a disgrace.

Moreover, Manne adduces considerable evidence to show that children attending child-care centres have higher stress hormone levels than children of comparable age being cared for at home. I'm not quite sure how to read the statistics, but for the time being they're worrying. I still believe that the provision of accessible, affordable, quality child-care must be a central component of any thrust towards women's advancement and a more caring society. But it's back to the drawing board; we have to do much better than we have.

Manne ends her essay with a wishlist of measures to help parents and children – those "working families" of the Labor Party mantra. Many of her ideas come from Scandinavian countries, long the models for progressive employment and family policies. The social-democratic, Scandinavian solutions are as attractive now as they were last century, and Scandinavian parents of very young children today can choose between high quality child-care and a home-care allowance. This, Manne contends, is the kind of "neutral policy" the Rudd government should adopt. But how neutral is it? A lot of money will be needed to revamp the child-care system, to establish the 260 child-care centres Rudd promised during the campaign, let alone the "one-stop centre" idea he put forward for the 2020 Summit. Will the choice Manne proposes mean, in the long term, no choice at all? The Scandinavian example relies on a network of child-care centres already established; in Australia that network, despite huge outlays in subsidies, has been effectively allowed to run down.

Her proposals for extended paid parental leave, part-time and flexible work, community centres for parents and children, improved quality of child-care, a decent wage for carers, higher accreditation standards and universal pre-school education all formed part of an earlier agenda, along with, most importantly, a shortened working week. All were swept away with the triumph of the market. Now some are gaining public acceptance again, and governments have even been taking up some of them. But, here too, the funding will have to come from somewhere, unless we are to rely too heavily yet again on private operators providing what should be, above all, a community service.

Which brings me full circle to my awakening in that Canberra office where I wrote the minister's speeches, and Anne Manne's grim serfdom on that outback station – experiences that took us to slightly different positions in what is virtually the same space. People at work have always needed a strong, enlightened union movement and truly responsive governments to protect them against ruthless employers and the ideologies that support them. The resounding rejection of WorkChoices is evidence enough of that. We also have to consider whether annual tax cuts and chest-thumping surpluses are the way to go. We have come to a point in our nationhood where it is imperative that collective solutions are given at least equal weight to individual ones, and that more and more women will take part in them. My differences with Manne are mere quibbles beside our common hope that the Rudd government will modify its fiscal conservatism and lead us back to the future.

Sara Dowse

Don Edgar

Anne Manne's *Love & Money* is an interesting, but incomplete, analysis of the ways in which, she believes, dramatic shifts in the "gender bargain" and "new capitalism" have altered the culture and demand new policies of family support.

Her proposals for reform, at the end of her essay, are hardly contestable – improved provisions for parental leave, job flexibility, child-care quality, community support services and universal pre-school. But there is a tone of fervour about motherhood that leads to overstatement and undermines her case. She is particularly concerned that attachment theory and separation anxiety need to be better understood, because we don't want "a baby – at the height of separation anxiety – spending up to ten hours per day in child-care. Only a bureaucracy could have designed a policy so insensitive to infant needs."

There is no monolithic policy or system of child-care "designed" by bureaucrats. Most child-care is private or community-based and parents make such a "choice" out of necessity – they have a mortgage to pay off, there's no one else to babysit, their employer demands a quick return to work, there's inadequate maternity leave or absence from the office will stymie a career.

Indeed, very few infants spend that sort of time in long day-care: 5 per cent of children aged below one, 21 per cent of children aged one to two (and not all of them are there for ten hours a day, every day). In fact, only 38 per cent of mothers with a baby under one are employed, mostly on a part-time basis.

Anne Manne acknowledges all this, yet blames bureaucrats, feminists, the "work-centred commentariat," "left-leaning progressives," "the child-care lobby," "an international network of activists determined to install the early child-care agenda," and those "shaping the cultural script." What a litany of culprits to explain why today's mothers "neglect" their children in the early years and go to work in a hedonistic pursuit of consumerism instead of staying home for years (as Anne Manne apparently did) to ensure proper "attachment" and "attunement," the basis of optimism and trust, "an emotional map of the world."

There is no study I know (and no study quoted in the essay) that shows children cared for full-time by mums (and for how long anyway: one, five or twenty years?) have a better "emotional map" than the majority who spend some time at least (not ten hours a day) in non-parental care. The main factor in children's wellbeing is the mother's satisfaction with her lot (whether working at home or in a paid job) and feeling that her partner does a fair share of the load. Few children throughout human history have had the luxury of full-time maternal care.

It is this evangelical tone that mars Manne's essay. Her own work experience while she was a jillaroo in outback New South Wales for "Mr and Mrs Slavedriver" is almost Dickensian. Poor Anne had to muster cattle before eight, "red dust clogging our boots and coating our skins," then feed slops to the cattle dogs, change nappies, cook every meal for the family and wash all the clothes. No wonder she stood "swaying, at the bottom of the hill," as her "burnt fingertips" (from re-used matches) strained to carry the heavy buckets. This is her evidence against feminist rhetoric about "the liberation of work" and apparently why she spent so many years in domestic duties before developing a career (as a money-earning writer and part of the elite workforce she admonishes).

I could embellish the description of my own widowed mother, swaying at the bottom of the hill as she started the walk to Fletcher Jones' factory in Warrnambool at 7.30 a.m., and then walking back to a family of five in need of feeding at around 6 p.m. But I know she enjoyed that work because it paid the bills, gave her a friendship support group and freed her from domestic boredom, not to mention that we older kids bucked in and helped with much of the feeding and caring for our younger siblings, vegetable growing, clothes washing, shopping and housework. Not all work is with a slavedriver boss, not all women are forced into a job and not all mums do the caring work alone. Nor was our "emotional map of the world" damaged by our mother's workplace focus and "neglect" of us during the long working days – in fact, we were caring for one another, at school, playing sport, as are most kids, not pining for more maternal comfort.

Along with a very selective use of sources, what is missing from Anne Manne's analysis is a sense of history about family life, trends which the Australian Institute of Family Studies (along with others) has documented thoroughly since its inception in 1980. For example, her concern that the caring work of women is not counted in our national accounts as part of GDP has been repeatedly expressed by Duncan Ironmonger of Melbourne University. Recognition of the value of caring work and equal contributions to marriage were built into the *Family Law Act 1975* provisions for property division and child maintenance. Various aspects of caring work have been costed by the Institute.

The move of Australian women back into paid work was well underway by the 1950s and is not just a product of feminism or neo-capitalism. British researcher Catherine Hakim was not the first to discover women had diverse attitudes to paid employment. Indeed, Hakim's research was more remarkable for the fact that it finally drew John Howard's attention to the blatantly obvious – that women were diverse, not universally focused on home-making – not for its innovation. It made a trite and misleading distinction between just three "types" of women: work-centred, home-centred and "adaptive" women (the majority). Their "preferences" change as their circumstances do. Howard had refused to listen, until it became clear the workplace needed women and the majority wanted paid work but had trouble because the male-dominated workplace had failed to adapt. WorkChoices did not quite fit the bill.

The issue of diversity and the cultural shift away from a single model of marriage and family was central to the work of the Institute of Family Studies – well before Anthony Giddens's work on the transformation of intimacy – and made a huge difference to social security and other policy areas. We were attacked by both Labor and Liberal parties for our AFIT (Australian Families Income Transfer) modelling of election tax promises to "help the family," modelling which showed how diverse family structures, sizes and economic needs were, yet our findings were later taken into account in revised policy settings.

Those arguing for better quality and more universal child-care were not motivated by wanting to push all mothers into paid work, but by the fact that mothers were returning to workplaces that refused to recognise their dual work and family responsibilities, and by the fact that child-care quality was not guaranteed. Reality, and the best interests of children who were in care, was the motivation. Far from being part of some monolithic child-care lobby, we fought with the ACTU over the failure of their maternity leave campaign to consider parental care. And we did major research on the impact of various forms of child-care on children's wellbeing, showing that low socio-economic status, ethnicity and maternal satisfaction with job versus home "choices" were more important than child-care in explaining child outcomes. The Institute's current longitudinal study of children will be of major interest in this regard.

The Australian Institute of Family Studies had also been calling for a more responsive workplace culture for years. Gradually we won over the Business

Council of Australia, several major companies developed better work/family cultures and small businesses formed consortiums to cover work/family problems in less costly ways.

Far from being an elite mouthpiece for a feminist agenda, the AIFS has been (during my tenure as director for fourteen years and since) an advocate for family support – not just child-care but every form of family care, including aged care, maternal and child health, family counselling and financial advisory services, more integrated children's services, decent housing, adequate family payments, maternity and parental leave, a workplace culture more responsive to family responsibilities and family-law reforms to ensure adequate child maintenance and more sensible post-divorce parenting arrangements.

Anne Manne calls for better family-support services, a more family-responsive workplace culture, an adequate parental leave system along the lines of Sweden or England (both of which found such leave was preferred by parents to placing their children too early in long day-care, even of high quality). I agree totally with all that, and with her correctly pointing out that the oft-quoted cost-benefit of $7 for every $1 spent in the Perry Pre-school Project cannot be generalised to all children in child-care. Most of us who use that figure use it as an illustration in support of better investment in early childhood services of every kind, without assuming it is the last word in research.

But her assertions about why women are working do not bear close examination. She fails to consider the key changes – couples who marry later have established career paths and/or economic needs; they have fewer children, so "time out" of the workplace decreases anyway (as opposed to her driving kids to school from the late 1980s to 2006, nearly twenty years); child-care is better linked now with other types of family-support services (as in Victoria's Children's Hubs); and, though belatedly, more workplaces have adapted to the family-related care responsibilities of employees they must competitively attract and retain.

She makes a fleeting reference to the coming demands of an ageing population, which may alter the dependency ratio and increase health costs. But she does not mention the fact that Australians over sixty-five contribute almost $39 billion to the national economy in unpaid work, nor discuss how mothering (of fewer children, later in life) will alter the nature of aged care itself. In my 2006 book The War Over Work: The Future of Work and Family, I discuss this in detail within the framework of better policy recognition of "caring work" – proposing a Carer's Wage, as opposed to narrowly targeted child-care payments and discrimination in favour of one type of family caring arrangement for children over another.

Anne Manne sets up straw men (and women) to misrepresent views that in fact support the policy thrust of her argument. She seeks to convert people to her cause – a particular form of motherhood is her religion. Perhaps one day research will examine how well these highly mothered young people deal with the challenges of their lives. Meanwhile, for most women we need policies and critiques that deal realistically with the ways families change, and how new technology and unfettered consumerism have altered the place of children in society, not the purple prose of Anne Manne's *Quarterly Essay*.

Don Edgar

May Lam

When our second baby was just eight weeks old, I would leave the house at 9 a.m., go to the office a fifteen-minute drive away, work for an hour and a half, drive home, feed the baby, drive back to the office and work till 2 p.m., watching the clock. Coming home I drove like a demon, cut in front of other cars and cursed the traffic. I had to know my daughter was alive.

That year I was haunted by a vague sense of dread that I would pay for this removal of myself. I don't think I thought of giving up work. Instead, to make it up to her I slept with the baby at night, feeding her on demand for the first year of her life. What was I thinking?

Anne Manne urges us to recognise the collective social madness that in its rush to promote paid work for women fails to acknowledge, honour and enjoy the bonds of mother and baby. That the recognition causes pain, mostly to mothers, is borne out by the furious responses when Manne aired these ideas several years ago. But Manne is merely recovering the original project of feminism: to give women access to the full spectrum of what it means to be human. In doing so, she has pointed out the tendency of any progressive social movement to stray from its original ideals and even to endorse forms of coercion.

Manne is the unflinching Cassandra of feminism and child-care debates. Prophetic in pointing to sorry truths about what the new capitalism is doing to the family, she is girded by an enviable moral conviction. This is particularly striking in an era of intellectual relativism, when the right to make personal choices is accorded automatic respect, even when the choices made can be bad for others.

The choices under capitalism, as Manne points out so bracingly, tend towards the getting of more. Whether it is more career advancement, more gadgets, more average housing square metres or more purchasing power to get the health and education security that seems to be slipping away, all we seem to want to do –

and urge on mothers – is work, work, work. What this means for babies and children is less time with their parents, with the worst consequences for development if the child is deprived of maternal attention in the first two years of life.

The texture of the argument is rich and diverse. Manne takes us to the school gate and the pronouncements of the OECD, to the mass media, the child psychologist and the long-day-care centre. The writing is peppered with emphasis added, exasperated exclamation marks, terms such as "experts" and "social inclusion" held at critical distance by being set in quotation marks. One senses that Manne is ready for battle, for the letters challenging her reporting and interpretation of the findings. But the battle is simply an invitation to parents to think differently about how much work they do, and for governments to offer them better choices.

Manne is on high moral ground in putting the case. Her 2005 book, *Motherhood*, opens with an account of the decision she made to raise her two daughters at home. This is a feminist voice we barely recognise, one that speaks of joy, pleasure and pride in mothering, not of the "problem with no name," not of "speaking bitterness." But it's not just feminism that might be unsettled by this pleasure principle. Could the State, too, come at funding mothers for such joyous work? This is the policy nub of the essay: if women choose to stay home to raise their children, they should receive a cash benefit, a home-care allowance equivalent to the cost of a child-care place.

It's a timely suggestion. At an Australian community-sector conference in April there was talk about how the government should fund, support and measure social inclusion (and in view of the evident sincerity and goodwill brought to the exercise, let's not always call it "social inclusion"). Not surprisingly, paid employment emerged as the desirable objective and dominant indicator. Still, the first speaker in the welfare-to-work stream wondered if work was overrated, and a more forceful case was put by advocates for unpaid care workers. They raised the spectre of all these carers being compelled to join the labour force, to be replaced at vastly greater expense to the State by low-paid care workers. "Whether it's a baby or a frail aged person who needs their bottom wiped," as someone there put it, "you know it had better be done by someone doing it for love."

Fair enough, but if we agree that the government has to be accountable for the money it spends, we might ask what performance or success measures would support the proposal for a home-care allowance? Women merely *leaving* the workforce? An increase in hours spent caring for children? Manne's evidence indicates that possible measures include children with lower stress levels or, in the longer term, better educated and better adjusted children. But the factors involved in these kinds of outcomes are complex, and, as Manne has pointed out herself, competing interests can distort the ways that forms of social good are measured. It seems the government would have to forego its generally reasonable need for an "outcome measure" in this particular case, since the positive benefit of a home-care allowance is the very choice itself.

Though the essay notes the alarming rate of fertility decline, other analysts have pointed out that this might be linked to the domestic division of labour at home as much as to the market conditions of new capitalism. In Italy (and other European countries), for example, a drop in fertility is significantly correlated with the division of labour at home, so that the more housework women are expected to undertake, the less they are likely to add to it by having more children. We might contemplate Project Homemaker for young men to promote women's interest in breeding, as well as greater financial and social recognition for mums.

I'd like to have seen what Manne had to say about dysfunctional mothering, and to consider the point at which poor mothering overtakes poor child-care in damaging children. On this difficult point, we might wonder whether a condition of getting the home-care allowance should be "good-enough" mothering, how this could be determined, and what the implications would be for mothers deemed not good enough.

The essay does not explore the evidence about what low-paid women want. Though like Manne I've seen "Get to Work" advocates among professional elites confusing their own job satisfaction and career advancement with what is good for low-income mothers, experience in labour-market programs in Australia and the UK shows that a significant minority of lone parents are extremely keen to work and will volunteer for programs to get a job. Interviewing some of these women, and sceptical myself about the satisfaction to be gained from minimum-wage service jobs, I have been struck by their reports of job satisfaction, pride in working, skills gained and focus on the goal of having a career. For these women, "getting out of the house" is valued and quite a few of them believe it makes them better mothers. It is also surprising, and enlightening, to learn that some workers identify positively with their place of employment and its corporate goals, showing off with some pride the workplaces to which they have gained access. These experiences worked against my own expectations.

Yet the satisfaction with work felt by some lone mothers should not be converted into a requirement for all of them to go into paid work. Parents themselves are best placed to determine what work they want and can manage, to assess how to calculate the journeys from home to school or child-care, to the workplace – which only *might* be flexible – and to do that with reference to the needs of their own particular children. Recognising these critical differences for each individual case, as Manne tells us, is the only basis on which lone parents might genuinely be supported to work in ways that will be good for them.

A few minor points. Though the Prime Minister and his wife are pleasing symbols of the modern couple, who demonstrate various patterns of stay-at-home and work life, I'd love to know how far 24/7 Kevin acknowledges the need for his staff and public servants to spend time with their families. I'd also like to know what Manne thinks of work-based child-care, though I suspect that she would see it as a case of Employer 1, Baby Nil in claims on the mother's time.

The essay's title, *Love & Money*, teasingly invokes a related question about choices women make about suitable fathers for their future children. Many women shrewdly consider a man's capacity to support her and the children they might have when sizing him up. Whether it is pride or prejudice, the dream of a rich husband endures. My own daughter has announced her intention to find such a one for herself, and perhaps this is a response to having had a working mother.

May Lam

Steve Biddulph

In her essay *Love & Money*, Anne Manne shows a depth and range of analysis that is rare in social-science writing today. Her arguments go behind the child-care debate, behind the work and family tension that is now in the foreground of most Australians' daily lives, to ask the really big question.

Are we, in spite of our relative affluence, becoming economic slaves, who must sacrifice essential human freedoms merely to be able to live? Or are we free, at least free enough, to have time for love, to be close, build families and develop communities sufficient to sustain us into a liveable future? It's hard to think of a question more central to every choice we make, as a nation and as individual human beings. Love takes time, and hurry is the enemy of love, eroding it and preventing its growth. When we hurry parents with economic pressures and a culture that only values earning and spending, we tear at the fabric from which healthy human beings are woven.

Child-development experts, myself included, have been cagey about pointing out two very large elephants in the living room of contemporary life. The first is that in terms of child-rearing ability, the capacity to raise intelligent, socially integrated and mentally healthy children, we have probably been going backwards for several hundred years. The hunter-gatherer peoples, who made the first 99 per cent of our history, survived by being some of the best parents on earth. Without fangs or claws, our species lived by social cohesion, communication, culture and intellect, and at its heart this meant transmitting nurturing abilities which if lost would mean extinction. I have studied the remnants of this culture across the Third World, from West Bengal to Papua New Guinea, and marvelled at the lovingness of the parents and the aliveness of the children. Some Tongan women I once spoke to expressed real horror that we would place a baby in a separate cot at night, let alone in a separate room. They regarded a baby's crying as something going badly wrong. What they would make of long day-care, or controlled crying, I shudder to think.

The second and very frightening consequence of this – the offspring elephant of the first, if you like – is that we are now creating mentally disabled young humans in epidemic – perhaps even dominant – numbers. ADHD, Asperger's, bipolar disorder, depressive and anxiety disorders, and their resulting addictive behaviours such as binge drinking or drug use, are now affecting 10 to 20 per cent of all young people. We now know that these disorders are developmental: they arise from a lack of the right experiences in the early weeks and months of life; they are disorders of attachment.

Canada's best-known psychiatrist, Gabor Mate, himself a Holocaust baby born in Nazi-occupied Hungary, has documented how brain development, 70 per cent of which must happen in the first five years of life, can be seriously impaired by parental stress. The regions of the brain that mediate calmness, self-soothing, emotional regulation, empathy for others, and also attending and focusing, can only be acquired if parents themselves possess these attributes and have time to pass them on. This transmission is very largely unconscious and automatic in the millions of small things that happy and settled parents naturally do with their child. The sudden epidemic of mysterious brain abnormalities is almost certainly the result of this disrupted parent–child interaction. We can blitz the child with medication, but the success is partial, temporary and sometimes harmful. We can ameliorate the deficiencies with love and care, but they are hard to undo.

Love is not a mystery to the neuroscientist. Its hormones, especially oxytocin, are clearly stimulated by touch, loving smiles, patient and attentive body language; and these things in turn stimulate the growth of the brain. Day-care staff of the best quality, fully aware they are being filmed and rated, only manage a fraction of the loving exchanges given by all but the most depressed mother or father. These exchanges, labelled "joint attention sequences," are the literal food of love, and they build the most advanced human cognitive skills we will ever acquire: the abilities to interpret, empathise with and manage the reactions of others, in fact to be able, by the late teens, to stand in another's shoes while still keeping a hold on one's own perspective. In short, to care about others as much as oneself. This is not just the highest level of cognitive development, it is the root of all successful couple, family and community life.

Young humans have suffered the loss of a number of primary ingredients of mental health as, over the last 150 years, our lives have moved further into the corporatised, individualistic way of life we now lead.

These losses can be summarised in four successive stages that have arrived like hammer-blows as we industrialised our lives. First, we lost our close daily contact with nature and its capacity both to develop our senses and soothe and integrate our mental state. (Pets, gardens and nature documentaries are about all we have left of this.) Secondly, we lost community: the network of caring, long-term relationships with people of several generations living in close proximity. Thirdly, we lost fatherhood: the strong and easy presence of men skilled at providing a male role model to boys and a positive masculine presence to girls. Finally, and most fatally, we are now seeing a decline of motherhood in the lives of children. (Anne Manne quantifies a clear reduction in the time children and teenagers spend with mothers or aunties or grandmothers. For girls in particular, this lack of real time has offset some of the gains of feminism in terms of self-esteem, hence the resurgence of eating disorders and anxiety about looks and image.)

These losses have not gone unnoticed, and there is considerable concern, based on sound research, about the devastating effects on child development. There are also pockets of good news: fathers have enjoyed a renaissance of late, almost trebling their time spent with children in the last thirty years. Parents themselves have begun to link up into a kind of resistance movement to the erosion of family and community. From the Australian Breastfeeding Association to Kids Free2B Kids (the very effective lobby group against the sexual commodification of children in advertising) and the federal government's overdue confrontation with the alcohol industry, this movement is wide and deep. Our children's future seems poised in the balance. As many as 60 per cent of mothers still resist returning to full-time work until their children reach school age. The group that researchers term "slammers" – those parents who put babies into full-time day-care from under the age of six months – are still a minority, less than one in twenty families. And paradoxically these tend to be largely the most affluent parents; low-income parents fight returning to work and only do so reluctantly and with much grief and stress. Immigrant and refugee parents from more nurturing cultures are horrified by the idea of stranger-care and only use it in cases of direst need.

There have always been people who do not value time spent with their children and abrogate their duty of care. The worry is that this approach is being forced onto others, by housing prices, petrol costs and government policies on taxation and income support. Hence the fierce debate about paid parental leave. Parental leave provisions have made family life liveable in all the progressive social democracies of Europe, without visible harm to their economies. That we consign such matters to the Productivity Commission, as if it's an economic and not a moral or sustainability question, speaks for itself.

Something isn't working. As Manne points out, today we spend two to three times more on the basics of life, and spend twice to three times as much of our time doing so, as fifty years ago. Yet we work harder and longer. Someone somewhere is growing rich on this. Of course, it doesn't help that we now expect a quarter-acre house when once the dream was for that area of lawn and a veggie patch. But even a frugal family is in trouble today.

The risk of enslavement of the many by the few has always lurked in human society. Where it was once created by swords, whips and iron chains, today it comes as a combination of fear of poverty, our own greed and aspirations, and the lack of supportive community to buffer our vulnerability. We feel all alone. But there is still hope, and in the coming economic troubles this hope might actually flourish. Our own choices, supported by a government that sees the value of human cohesion and nurturing, might lead us to a devolution from a globalised to a human scale of living, where we live by caring more and consuming less and are richer for it.

Steve Biddulph

Virginia Haussegger

She is not the ogre she might seem, but that doesn't stop a number of women I know avoiding contact with Anne Manne. They don't want to discuss her, don't want to listen to her, and keep her book *Motherhood* at the bottom of their reading pile. It's a bit like going to the gym: they know they should do it for the sake of their health, but exercise requires a shifting of priorities – and so does reading Manne. She guilts women into feeling they must rethink their choices.

As one corporate high-flyer and new mother said to me recently when I spotted Manne's book gathering dust under her bed, "I had to stop reading it. I'm about to go back to work and put Jack in day-care. I already feel like a bad mother. She's freaking me out!"

As a non-mother I have no such reason to be threatened by her. But that's not to say Manne doesn't worry me. She does. And her *Quarterly Essay* worries me a lot. But let me be clear. Far from shooting the messenger, I want to applaud Anne Manne – thunderously. We need to hear her and we desperately need to have this discussion. Frankly I wish this gently spoken, considered and thoughtful woman would occasionally yell through a megaphone, so that more would take note.

What worries me most is that much of what Manne argues is right. I take issue with aspects of her argument, and will come to that. But, in short, Manne is arguing for a social revolution and she is right to do so. We do need to raise the place of children in our lives, if women are to go on having them. And we need to raise the value of mothering, if women are to continue doing it. We also need to look beyond economic measures and the GDP as indicators of Australia's general wellbeing. However – and this is where it gets tricky – attempting to devalue the personal and emotional benefits of paid work, or the satisfaction derived from "competitive achievement," isn't going to fix the problem, or help find foot-soldiers for the much needed revolution. Women enjoy and crave the challenges of demanding and interesting work just as much as men – let's not forget that.

I'd like to say that somewhere in Manne's drubbing of the "sanctification" of work and the glorification of child-rearing is a "middle-path" approach. But as it stands in Australia right now, it would seem women need to either love being at home with young children, or love being at work without them. Personally I don't think either is true. I suspect there are times when women both love it and hate it – on the same day. Which is why I don't have a problem with the model put forward by British sociologist Catherine Hakim.

As Manne points out, Hakim believes women fall into three general categories. A small percentage will always be fully career-focused, and an equally small percent will always be "home-centred." The biggest group in the middle will be "adaptive," that is, they like a bit of both worlds: working and raising children. Those women accommodate that dual pull by restructuring their work hours around family needs until their kids are older and they can work more. Hakim's overview is neither radical nor necessarily conservative. In fact, like Anne Summers, her analysis strikes me as "bleeding obvious." Nevertheless, when the Howard government invited Hakim here five years ago for a lecturing tour of Australia, there were rumblings of protest. The reasons were more to do with Hakim's perceived attack on feminists for being "dictatorial" about women's choices than with what she was here to say.

And this, too, is where Manne runs into trouble – on the issue of choice. Her strong advocacy for mothers to stay at home full-time with their children, at least during their infancy, has dictatorial overtones. Women don't like that. Already battered and bruised by the myriad contradictions they face when contemplating how they might juggle having a baby, raising a family and keeping a foothold in the world of work, many new mothers don't want to hear about the dangers of long hours in child-care. Just as hungry career aspirants with big ambitions don't want to hear the sound of their fertility window creaking shut.

Manne's *Quarterly Essay* discussion of the under-reported and often ignored data on the effect of long hours in child-care, on toddlers and babies in particular, is startling stuff. The high levels of the stress hormone cortisol found, even in children in high quality care, must surely alarm all parents. As should the evidence Manne cites about retarded development and learning difficulties. Even though I would have thought much of this was – to quote Summers again – "bleeding obvious." I mean, wouldn't any parent assume that touching, holding, loving, sharing, smiling and being joyous with babies is necessary for their healthy development, their sense of security and their ability to form intimate attachments? Perhaps not.

The "scare" element in what Manne has to say about child-care is strong. Is it a "tactic"? No, it's a truth: a most uncomfortable one. And for that, Manne will be ignored by some who don't want to hear it, and shouted down by others who don't like it. Like Manne I too have been accused of running something of a scare campaign, when I went public about my own battle with age-related infertility. While frightening young women into a "get breeding" regime was the last thing on my mind, I nevertheless feel all the public thrashing I received was worth it each time a young woman tells me she read my articles, or book, and now has a baby, or is thinking about it. Sometimes the use of scare tactics – albeit unwittingly – is what's required to jolt some serious review about priorities, and what matters most.

Manne is right about the very vexed nature of women's so-called "choice." I have been astounded and dismayed at how brutally we bludgeon women over the head with that ugly phrase, "Well, it was your choice." By throwing these profound life-cycle issues of fertility, family, child-care and career interruption back at women as if these are private matters to be grappled with behind a closed kitchen door alone, can be extremely isolating. Worse – many women wallow around in that isolation, beating up on themselves when they don't cope well and their various needs collide. In my travels interviewing women about their fertility choices, I found that never once did a woman look beyond her own private world for some kind of help to make sense of the various life collisions. The lack of structural supports, and the paucity of policy to help accommodate these important life choices, didn't seem to feature in women's thinking. While many spoke of work cultures that paid much lip-service to "flexibility" and "family friendliness," none of them really expected – or got – substantive support.

The workplace's intolerance of absence became more apparent the longer women stayed at home with their children. Those who chose full-time home mothering for more than a couple of years became sadly disillusioned with their careers and the considerable investments they'd made in them. While Manne is right to suggest the marginalisation of women in the workforce is something "usually shrugged off as one of life's inevitable compromises," the dreadful thing is it's not just men but women who are doing the shrugging. I repeatedly heard women sigh and say, "But, it was my choice." Yet, the sentiment that perhaps made my skin crawl most was the old nugget, "Well, someone's got to do it," when speaking about caring for a young family and managing a household.

And this is where I find myself at odds with Anne Manne. Yes, motherhood has long been devalued – no question about that. Yes, women pay a high price for making the choice to stay at home with their children. Yes, child-care has become increasingly commercialised, and for some even profitable. Yes, the true "worth of a wife" has become more apparent as women join the workforce (yet that has done nothing to improve her status). And yes, the "care penalty" for caring for others, be it elderly or children, is harsher than ever. And yet what concerns me most is that, at the core of all this, is a strange apathy – from women. Manne doesn't address this.

Early in her essay, Manne makes her case against the American feminist Linda Hirshman quite clear. And while far from wanting to be branded a "local Hirshmanite," a re-reading of that noisy woman's now infamous 2005 essay in the *American Prospect* is worth the trouble. Sure, Hirshman is shrill, and her Rules are silly. Instructing women to have no more than one baby; to "marry down" or marry young as "younger men are potential high-status companions"; and to embrace the power of money by losing "their capitalism virginity" as soon as they leave college, is part humour and part polemical rant. Women can see through that. But as in many polemics, once you wade past all the screaming headlines, into the body of what she has to say, there is a sobering message. That message, to put it in the Antipodean vernacular, is simply this: men are getting away with blue murder, and women are letting them.

Hirshman has clearly never been into the boardroom of an Australian corporation. So when she says, "the public world has changed, albeit imperfectly, to accommodate women among the elite," she is being way, way too kind. However, she is on to something when she says, "[but] private lives have hardly budged." Then she hits a potent mark with this stinging claim: "The real glass ceiling is at home."

Hirshman quite rightly frets about feminism stalling. While she is specifically interested in the "opt-out" generation – those well-educated, well-heeled young college graduates who can afford to stay at home, cook pies and raise kids – her focus on the failure of feminism to radically change the domestic world is valid and pertinent to Australia.

Why are almost all the women I know still doing the lion's share of domestic work, when most of them are equally or more highly professionally qualified than their men? Is it because the role of attending to the home chores, the household management and the raising of young children is the sole province of women? Is domesticity inherently female?

One of the women I interviewed for my book almost spat at me when I posed this last question. Maya was an aspiring QC whose career was "on hold." She was folding underpants at the kitchen table as we spoke: "It's the most thankless, god-awful existence. I never wanted this role. I hate housework. I hate being at home. It's completely toxic."

Not everyone, it seems, can be lulled by the joyousness of being at home with toddlers. Not when they've had a taste of how intoxicating career adrenalin can really be. Right now, I have no idea how we can make folding the washing feel more fruitful. But I do suspect we can do an awful lot more to bring men into the mix. This is where the revolution needs to go. To that end, Manne's essay should serve as a good, solid kick-start.

Virginia Haussegger

Julie Stephens

In *Love & Money* Anne Manne calls on us to imagine a radically different model of social and political life, one that centres around care rather than on gendered notions of the autonomous, unencumbered individual. In this new social imaginary, care-giving would be recognised as thoughtful, intentional and moral work and human dependency be acknowledged as an inevitable part of the lifecycle. However, the kind of individualism currently reaping economic and social rewards is based on a denial of human dependency. The goal is to push towards an increasingly individuated self, perfectly tailored for the demands of the flexible labour market. According to Manne, this produces an "extreme worker norm" which operates as a covert form of discrimination by concealing a shadow economy of (largely) female care.

The broader philosophical questions underpinning *Love & Money* about selfhood, justice and moral action distinguish this *Quarterly Essay* from the divisive politics of the so-called mother wars and the tired accounting characteristic of the work/family balance debate. Manne's essay is also a thoroughly feminist intervention. It does not inflict a single, normative standard on women. It tackles questions of power, subordination and domination, arguing that the harsh penalties imposed by neo-liberal policies on those engaged in care-giving labour damage the least advantaged in our society: children, the frail elderly, mothers both in the workforce and at home, and poor immigrant women working in domestic labour and child-care. While Manne argues the problem is partly due to the dominance of a particular version of feminism – the liberal feminism that linked the emancipation of women with paid work – a different kind of feminism, that of the ethics of care tradition, is part of the solution.

There is no doubt that despite the rising demands of a globalised labour market, most of us will still spend a significant part of our lives giving care to dependents. Many will feel that that time was not long enough. Few, I think will look back at that period and consider it time wasted. We will also have significant phases in our lives where we require care and are unable to reciprocate. Whether as adults this appears in the form of illness, accident, lack of employment, gender disadvantage or eventually age, the idea of being dependent has strong emotive associations and a powerful pejorative charge. According to Nancy Fraser and Linda Gordon, being dependent was considered normal in pre-industrial times. It was viewed as a social relation based on the widespread recognition that everyone relied on someone else for survival. By contrast, dependency is now considered deviant and shameful, an individual and particularly feminised condition with psychological dimensions. Men engaged in sustained caring work, such as stay-at-home fathers or sons looking after elderly parents, are not only tainted by this stigma but also have to contend with work-centred notions of masculinity. As Manne repeatedly asks, how can we have gender equality around care and more just social relations if care-giving and dependency continue to be both socially undesirable and economically damaging?

According to Richard Sennett, all forms of dependency, on the state, employer, spouse or family, have become stigmatised in the new economy. Sennett characterises neo-liberalism as culturally opposed to the "dignity of dependence," requiring everyone, including the elderly, to act like stockbrokers or consultants in striving for an impossible ideal of self-sufficiency. The seductive force of this ideal especially impacts on those giving and receiving care. This is particularly evident in the writings of new mothers who document the shock of finding themselves relegated to the margins and feeling they have "returned to some primitive, shameful condition," as Rachel Cusk comments in *A Life's Work: On Becoming a Mother*. Maternity is experienced as acutely threatening to the clearly individuated self. The perception of losing autonomous forms of selfhood is also a powerful disincentive for new fathers. As argued in *Love & Money*: "Individualism and the new capitalism as value systems give men no real incentive to change." Without a thoroughgoing reorganisation of contemporary work practices and strong incentives for women and men to engage in "love's labour," such as the parental leave arrangements advanced by Manne, an unequal gender regime will be maintained.

There is a widespread cultural unease with maternalism evident in some of the responses to *Love & Money*. Explicitly maternalist voices are distinctly absent from the public domain. This seems truer in Australia than elsewhere. Women's claims as *workers* are acceptable, not their claims as *mothers*. This is puzzling on two counts. First, maternalism was a powerful political configuration in Australia from the late nineteenth century onwards and certainly contributed to the formation of the welfare state, which included women's hospitals, child endowment paid to mothers, infant and maternal welfare clinics and similar advances. My second point is based on my recent research into oral history accounts of the early women's liberation movement in Australia. What is clear in these records is that many of the campaigns of the 1970s were maternalist in the broad sense by transforming issues affecting mothers and children (such as domestic violence) from the private domain into public policy.

The oral history record also shows that early key Australian feminists had wide-ranging and alternative ideas about child-care that could not be further removed from the ABC Learning corporate model. It is possible then that the dominance of a *work-centred* liberal feminism is a much more recent phenomenon than previously thought. How did we move from ideals of co-operative, small-scale neighbourhood arrangements for infants and children to the almost nineteenth-century 'babies rooms' of contemporary commercial child-care centres? Rudd's idea of a one-stop shop for infants and children, where extended drop-off times for parents can be even more efficiently managed and reduced, further reinforces a social arrangement where paid work is the key value: shop is the operative word here.

Manne argues that nurture and care should be at the forefront of our policy and ethical agendas. This directive does not exclude fathers or men and women who have not had children. In my view, maternal forms of selfhood are not the preserve of mothers but emerge and flourish when people are engaged in care-giving, regardless of gender. Why then is the maternal such a deeply contested cultural space? *Love & Money* takes a different path to that of reproducing the fiction of a self-sufficient individualism on which the culture of neo-liberalism is founded. It presents policy alternatives to the existing social and economic penalties imposed on those giving care and tries to speak for those who are dependent. Without exception, one day, this will include all of us. Clearly, it is time to think about a new social imaginary around care.

Julie Stephens

Sushi Das

In *Love & Money* Anne Manne argues we are at a fork in the road: an historic turning point in the dance between work and family. The workplace has become the
arena of women's liberation, pushing feminism straight into the hands of capitalism's need to get everyone into work. When paid work is sanctified, motherhood is devalued and this does feminism no favours, she says. So we have a
choice: we can carry on celebrating individualism and self-sufficiency while
bludging off women who provide unpaid care for others; or we can create a new
system where care for others is deemed as important as paid work and people
recognise their interdependence. Manne is optimistic that under a Rudd government we can create a fairer social arrangement.

She is passionate and persuasive in bringing together many strands: the relationship between feminism and capitalism, what women want, what children
need, the relentless pressure on women to juggle work and family, and how the
commentariat is in step with the prevailing orthodoxy that women must get
back to work for the good of the economy and that child-care is necessary for
this to happen. Ultimately, she calls for a new way of thinking, one where government policy is neutral and women are neither forced into paid work, nor left
with no choice but to stay at home. Everyone should read her essay, especially
men.

The problem is not so much that there are a significant number of women
devaluing motherhood by buying in to the current work model, but that too
many men are devaluing motherhood by perpetuating that system. Clearly men
are either failing to effect change or are simply ignoring the work/family imbalance as a "women's issue." While I agree with much of what Manne so elo-
quently argues, I think she says little about the role of men and the fact that they
must be an essential part of the conversation if anything is to change. We simply
can't carry on talking about the burden that women continue to carry in the

twenty-first century without calling men to account. Crudely speaking, this does not mean we have to be anti-men; rather, men need to be included in any examination of what a better future might look like.

A few weeks ago I was in a taxi driven by a 26-year-old man. Taxi drivers are by no means representative of the voice of young men in the Western world, but this particular driver's comments were insightful. We struck up a conversation about work and he complained that in Australia all we ever do is work, work, work, for insufficient pay. He would probably have two children in his thirties, he said confidently, just as soon as he achieved a sound financial footing. He had no partner, but predicted that the mother of his children would probably work part-time. I said I was contemplating whether to work part-time so I could spend more time caring for my toddler. "If your boss lets you, I reckon you should work part-time," he said. "Take a few years, put your feet up. You might not get another chance."

Now I know there is no clinically proven therapeutic effect from a hard blow to the head, but I was sure that in his case it would at least wake him up. The idea that looking after children at home is not actually work is so deeply ingrained in some people that it's hard to know what it might take to induce a mind-set change. Yet that is precisely what is required: a massive mind-set change. The need for it is not confined to men: our political leaders, our employers, even women who think they must behave like men (but seldom decent ones), require it too.

But how far have we come? Despite the remarkable strides that have been made in the fight for equality, the recent shift affecting all Western societies – a new paradigm, as Manne puts it – is to see economic advantages in increasing women's participation in the workforce. So women are ordered to get back to work, preferably full-time, for the good of the economy; to produce children to counter the declining birth-rate; to raise these children in an increasingly complex and fast-moving society, or pay someone else to look after their children – and all this while governments and employers barely lift a cynical finger to help balance child-rearing and work.

"What is so striking among the partisans for the Get to Work program is the breathtaking complacency with which they regard state coercion," writes Manne. "Women's autonomy over balancing work and family – such intimate matters as birthing, breastfeeding, the speed of physical and psychological separation of mother and child and the timing of the return to work – is treated with blithe disregard." Same old problem, new shackles.

Some women want to work and rear children not just because they want to pursue the careers in which they have already invested so much time but because they want to benefit from the stimulation and rewards that come with paid employment. There is no shame in that. Others work because they have no choice. They have to pay the mortgage and the bills and they understand the need to contribute to superannuation. But whether they are middle-class mothers or working-class mothers trying to manage work and family, governments have repeatedly failed them by doing nothing about the shocking state of child-care in Australia (sorry, but a legal minimum ratio of one child-care worker to five children is unforgivably delinquent) and by failing to provide any statutory support for women leaving work to have children. These are just two areas that need to be overhauled.

And who are the people constantly complaining about these issues, placing them in the spotlight, screaming for change, tearing their hair out in frustration? Women. Where are men? The fathers? The husbands? The current work/family imbalance affects men as much as it does women. The same goes for the declining birth-rate, the pressure on motherhood, disgraceful child-care, the ongoing battle for gender equality and the future of feminism. Men, too, have to argue that it's time to recognise the contribution that women are making in work and child-rearing. By doing so they do not denigrate their own contribution in the arena of paid work. Indeed, their voices would help to lift the burden on their own shoulders. Equality is about men and women. As Fay Weldon said: "There has to be a halt in the gender war and feminism must extend its remit to include the rights of men."

Ironically, by failing to engage in issues broadly relating to the work and family in sufficient numbers and without sufficient force, men are doing what women have done for too long: policing their own oppression. In the sphere of work alone, men can make changes to break down the macho culture of their own making. That's just one step. For example, men don't have to get to work earlier than the start of their shift to impress the boss, nor stay late to look committed. Every additional hour at work is an hour away from the family. Men should not subject each other to subtle pressures that reinforce the ethos that long hours are what you do if you're a real man. They should commend each other for leaving the office on time instead of invoking guilt and perpetuating the idea that long hours are the only way to the top.

Men who are senior enough to negotiate individual work contracts should include provisions for a sensible work/life balance. Employers who say they are keen to promote family-friendly workplaces should be held to account in these contracts. Male managers who are asked by their bosses to increase productivity, which inevitably means longer hours for the men junior to them, should resist the pressure on behalf of their colleagues. Furthermore, a gender gap in terms of equal pay means men are often the bigger earners. Women frequently reshape their work life around the needs of children, partly to keep the larger income flowing in. There are fathers, I'm sure, who at some stage might like to reshape their work life around their children but don't because it makes less financial sense. Pay parity with women would surely make this easier for them. Attitudinal changes towards balancing work and family have to start in the hearts of educated men in senior positions – the men who are already on the A-list. Anything less perpetuates their own exploitation, as well as that of women.

Manne is right to point out that feminism gains its moral authority from being universal – on behalf of all women – but that it loses this authority when it acts on behalf of sectional interests. She illustrates this point with the example of highly educated, well-paid elites who decide for other women what their interests might be and advocate on their behalf. This is fair enough, but I would also argue that it is just as damaging for feminism to fail to scoop up men, carry them along on the journey to equality and prod them to realise they have work ahead. In time, employers and governments will have to stop basing their decisions on the backward-looking model of man-as-breadwinner and woman-as-child-rearer. (I can't believe it's 2008 and there is still a need to write a sentence like that.) Men now, and into the future, face the big problem of adjusting to their new and rather complicated roles. That problem is likely to be resolved when men and women are treated as workers and as parents, and given real choices.

Manne has written an important essay, which, more than anything else I have read recently, makes an engaging and intelligent contribution to a debate central to our lives. She describes how Kevin Rudd and his wife Therese Rein are symbolic of the modernisation of the Australian family. She makes a reasoned and urgent call for adopting policies similar to those in more progressive countries such as Britain and Sweden. She is hopeful that change might start under a Rudd government. I hope she is right but I am less optimistic, as I think it is still early days. Manne's essay should start a debate and it will be interesting to see the extent to which men engage with it. Certainly, her essay should be essential reading for one man – the Prime Minister.

Sushi Das

Natasha Cica

The publication of Anne Manne's *Quarterly Essay* on the family and the free market was well timed. It hit news-stands just as it was becoming clear, several months after federal election 07, that in important respects Kevin Rudd's unfurling social and economic blueprint for Australia is very different from John Howard's.

One point of difference should prove to be a readiness to pull policy levers to make it easier for Australians who either have or want children to negotiate a healthier, happier space between the twin tugs of Care and Mammon. This I understood to be the core of Manne's argument. She rightly pointed out that this will demand payment of more than lip-service to notions of choice and work–life balance, and real recognition that neo-liberalism isn't all it's cracked up to be. She closed her essay by presenting a wishlist of twelve suggestions to further these aims. These suggestions deserve consideration, especially her urgings to improve the quality of child-care and to learn lessons from European (particularly Scandinavian) parental-leave initiatives.

I hope that the manner and form of that consideration will play a part in establishing another key point of difference between the Howard and Rudd eras. One of the hallmarks of the former was a tendency to characterise positions that did not match the government's agenda as "elite" (this was not meant as a compliment) and to caricature those advancing them as members of the "commentariat" (ditto). Accompanying this was not inconsiderable resistance to the participation of women, especially pre-menopausal ones, in debates on matters *not* connected with their reproductive capacity … unless their published persona was gung-ho neo-con, which tended to bring rapid career rewards relative to merit. The triple whammy was that smart women expressing opinions about Australia's revived population anxiety soon realised they'd walked into a particularly toxic cul-de-sac of the culture wars – a kind of naked mud-wrestling bout with footnotes.

Manne apparently acknowledged this last fact in the introduction to her essay, lamenting the "intolerant atmosphere of the interminable mother wars." It was disappointing, then, to see slogans like "commentariat" and "elite cultural script" cranked out too many times in the following pages. In an echo of past habit, these labels were pinned only on positions with which Manne disagreed.

Or imputed positions. I was surprised to find my own name on Manne's hit list, both as a "work-centred careerist" preoccupied with the so-called baby versus briefcase dilemma, and as a member of the commentariat, "most of whom are themselves leading that life." Beyond that, I allegedly hold "contempt for stay-at-home mothers."

All that was a very wild stretch of Manne's imagination. My May 2007 column from which Manne selectively quoted wasn't dumping on women who, like Therese Rein and most Australian mothers, spend time out of the paid workforce caring for their children. Rather I was using the Rudd/Rein "appendage" furore to make a larger democratic point about what was and wasn't getting due attention in the lead-up to November's federal election. Here's the relevant passage:

> The intense speculation surrounding the business affairs of Therese Rein, and their potential political implications for prime ministerial contender Kevin Rudd, probably reveal more about us than about either of them.
>
> It suggests we've turned into a nation of voyeurs, alive and reactive to any deviation from prevailing norms. "Reining her in" and "Firm grip on rudder," the headlines have tittered since Rein announced her decision to divest local operations. Granted, it's not the average Australian wife – certainly not the average Australian political wife – who has the entrepreneurial drive and talent to set up a booming global business, never mind referring to it on the record as her "life support."
>
> Then again, it's not the average middle-aged Australian woman who's also a cheerfully practising Christian, evidently still happily married (but not joined at the hip) to the man she met at university, and clearly satisfied with the balance she's struck between family and fortune.
>
> Having said that, in many respects Rein is pretty stock standard – most able-bodied Australian mothers work, or they want to. As is

her husband – most able-minded Australian men don't want a dependent appendage and are prepared to stand up and say so. So why the fevered commentary pitch?

One reason might be that it's still not crystal clear why Rein and Rudd didn't have their private pow-wow on conflict of interest before it blew up in their faces. The reason may never be revealed, especially now both parties must surely be supersensitive to the dangers of one misplaced public utterance, like the politically incorrect "appendage." But do we really need to know this?

Without evidence of any intention to wilfully deceive the public – Rein and Rudd have hardly kept the Ingeus empire and its government contracting secret – it's hard to see there's any meaningful issue, especially as earlier this month Rein explicitly flagged her intention to seek advice on this matter from the head of the Department of the Prime Minister and Cabinet should Rudd be elected, and further to give the new opposition leader a chance to review any suggested probity arrangements. [...]

Every word from every bylined commentator and ranting blogger this week about Rein was a space that wasn't devoted to issues that should matter a whole lot more to Australians in an election year, like, say, the policies on offer.

Announcing Quentin Bryce as Australia's next governor-general, Kevin Rudd emphasised that the appointment was "a great reflection on the fact that modern Australia is about the proper role of women in our society, unconstrained." That was a substantial, and welcome, break from both long tradition and recent Australian practice. Not least because Bryce is widely admired for elegantly combining her more private roles (as wife, friend, mentor, mother of five and grandmother of more) with her professionalism (as lawyer, academic, feminist, human-rights advocate, federal sex-discrimination commissioner, National Childcare Accreditation Council chief executive, Women's College principal at the University of Sydney, and governor of Queensland). This might just herald the dawn of a classier, more collaborative chapter in Australian public life.

Natasha Cica

Anne Manne

Late one night over dinner, I listened to an ambitious young couple talk about life after the birth of their child. The mother-to-be had an intensely imagined scenario of equal work and sharing of care. The father-to-be vaguely agreed, but admitted he hadn't yet had much time to think about it as he had been working sixteen-hour days in a high-flying job. He was proud of the fact.

Admirable as the young woman's plan sounded, I was dubious that life would pan out quite the way she wanted. Sadly, such was the case: it turned out that her partner's new gender ideology was a veneer covering a much more power-ful ideal born of the new capitalism: the extreme worker norm.

Feminists have often, correctly, pointed out that the old ideology of the homemaker was a product of the old capitalism; the bleak world of the male fac-tory worker was supported by the "angel in the house" who provided a haven in a heartless world. The culture that installed the "cult of motherhood" was born of an economic system which required not women's autonomy over these matters, but women's submission to the norms which supported it.

In Love & Money my intention was to show how the new capitalism is remaking motherhood – and, by implication, all care-giving activity – along very different lines. At the same time, it too requires women's submission to the dictates of the economy. Long before we arrive at the terrain of women's preferences on work and family, agendas have been set.

The high quality of almost all of the contributions to this correspondence shows how important it is to have this conversation. Most raise valuable points that help refine it. Most understand the need to go beyond the narrowed and overheated confines of the mother wars. It is especially encouraging to read Julie Stephens, whose attentive reading of the recent and vibrant feminist scholarship on care enables her to grasp what is really at stake here: the larger issue of how our free-market society handles the question of care. It is heartening to see so many from different generations – Sara Dowse and Sushi Das, for example – engaging in such thoughtful and respectful discussion. And to have Steve Biddulph refuse to allow the question to be simply about the desires of adult men and women, but to include his passion, the wellbeing of children.

There is some suggestion in the correspondence that I wrote my book *Motherhood* from the perspective of a mother at home. No, I didn't, nor *Love & Money*. Instead they were born of reflection on the subject of care after both being at home with small children and spending an even longer period working in a two-career family. In this latter phase I experienced first-hand the challenges of answering the ethic of care while meeting the ever-expanding demands of the work I loved; responsibilities which increasingly included my mother's elder care and decreasingly my children's care, as they gained independence. I have been on both sides of this fence, and that is one reason the argument cuts across ideological divides. I came to the view, standing back from the fray, that a single issue is at stake in the difficulties women face: the devaluation of care. Mothers both in and out of the workforce are harmed by the care penalty.

Haussegger says she knows women who tremble to read me. I find this talk of guilt rather overblown and even infantilising. Aren't mothers at home or working part-time made to feel guilty by the much harsher critiques by the likes of Linda Hirshman?

My case was gently enough put. I argued that notwithstanding instances of depressed or inadequate parenting, caring for children is a good and worthwhile thing to do. The essay presented a modest, nuanced and measured case – sticking to the evidence – to show that child-care is not always what it is cracked up to be. And while acknowledging that the literature on child-care risk should not be catastrophised, it supported current parental behaviour and preferences, not the Get to Work program of ideological zealots.

In the course of publicising *Love & Money*, the word I so often encountered was "relief." Someone was talking about the *real* dilemmas people faced, and presenting alternatives. I do not claim that these readers of the essay agreed with every word. What I have discovered, however, is that the case I am making has a very large constituency. In fact, I would go so far as to say that it is only the true hardliners of gender fundamentalism on one hand, and the Get to Work ideologues on the other, who are truly suspicious of it. In the broad program I advocate, of longer parental leaves, of improved child-care and the larger project of revaluing care, all but a few can find themselves.

Sushi Das, in a thoughtful and intelligent response, wants me to talk more explicitly about men. I cannot, in an essay with limited space, cover everything;

I concentrated on women because the subject is care, and they do more of it. However, her larger question, of why, is crucial. The whole essay, as Julie Stephens understands, is about the deeper question of why women still do more care-work than anyone else, and what to do about this. I could have joined those uttering the "Men must do more!" exhortations which, judging by their results, have not got us very far. Or I could have penned yet another column on the work/life balance, to join those already gently drizzling down on us from the opinion pages.

Or I could cut to the chase. *Why* do work and family conflict? *Why* do so many mothers dramatically cut back or stay at home in the first couple of years? *Why* have roles of men changed so little?

The new capitalism creates contradictions in women's traditional role by valuing paid work and devaluing family work. The situation for men is very different. The fetishisation of paid work *undermines* women's traditional roles but *reinforces* men's. Even men with egalitarian ideals now often work longer hours than the traditionalist dads of the 1950s, home at five o'clock.

Neo-liberalism ties virtue and pride to economic self-sufficiency, but self-doubt and even shame to care-giving and dependency. Nowhere is this more pertinent than when speaking of men. Our judgment of stay-at-home dads – as opposed to those taking brief breaks between high-profile positions – is at least as harsh. The social judgments about men who fail to succeed at work are savage: "loser," "no-hoper," "deadbeat dad" and so on. Men are still very much judged according to their position in the labour market, more than by their performance as fathers.

Almost all discussions about men and care begin at the end-point – wondering why the flow of care from men is no more than a trickle – when, as Julie Stephens shows so well, we must travel upstream to the very source. There we would find that male energies and time have already been diverted, pouring into a vibrant and fast-flowing torrent called work.

Most people are open to a discussion that encompasses these root-and-branch questions, including a critical consideration of child-care. There is one exception to this in the correspondence. Don Edgar's contribution is dispiriting in its aggressive tone of partisanship. He consistently fails to rise to the occasion on this issue. Edgar finds nothing in what I present on child-care to concern him. Really? Nothing in a ratio of one caregiver to five babies? Even Eddy Groves, head of ABC Learning, has admitted that is too low. Edgar recalls one of the people described by Martin Krygier in his book *Civil Passions*, who deploy every means at their disposal to "block conversations rather than further them. The sort of conversational contribution that the American novelist Ring Lardner had in mind in a character's response to a question from his son. 'Shut up,' he explained."

Edgar insists on the ecumenical nature of the Australian Institute of Family Studies under his directorship. Unhappily, he cannot seem to talk about stay-at-home mothers without making their impact on their children sound foul ("highly mothered"). In order to make a point about the differences across the class divide over the meaning of work, I tell a story about being exploited as a teenager during a holiday job working sixteen-hour days on an outback station, and how it gave me, ever after, an insight into the ambiguous and shifting meanings of work. Because the teenager in question grew up to be part of what for Edgar is a hated group − stay-at-home mothers − the ex-director of the AIFS sneers and relishes the exploitation. He contrasts my attitude with that of his own heroic working mother − except that she was in a unionised factory working an eight-hour day protected by legislation. I was half her age and worked twice as long in a position unprotected by any union.

This is a point well grasped by Sara Dowse. The type of labour conditions I experienced, under neo-liberal policies, even without WorkChoices, are becoming more common, not less − like a café worker I know who is on her feet for seven hours straight, with no rights to meal or toilet breaks. When she sits down for fifteen minutes to eat, she is docked $2.50 from her $10 an hour wage. Dowse is right. However did we come to the view that unions were no longer necessary?

That said, Edgar's response is extremely valuable. This is because he candidly admits that the much-quoted mantra − $1 invested in child-care brings a $7 return − is false. He admits that I am right to debunk the claim, that he knows it to be false, *but that he uses it anyway.* I hope every policy-maker in the country, especially Kevin Rudd and Maxine McKew, reads that sentence. As Bruce Fuller points out, the Perry Pre-school Project, from which the figure was derived, involved very small numbers of children. That means some of the results, on the basis of which policy-makers and economists around the world are investing billions of taxpayer dollars, have been derived from studies of no more than ten children!

The willingness, among people who know better, to put that figure forward while knowing it to be false when applied to ordinary Australian child-care, has done enormous damage. It is used not as it should be − to help disadvantaged populations − but in the service of a very different aim: promoting universal child-care from zero to five. Barbara Romeril, for example, executive director of

Community Childcare Victoria, quoted the figure on *Lateline* as the basis of her claim that we know from overseas research that child-care gives children the best start in life. No qualifications were offered. Even Rudd has used the figure Edgar and I both know to be false. But how is Rudd to know any better if people like Edgar, carrying the imprimatur of taxpayer-funded institutions like AIFS, don't tell him? It is quite simply one of the great social policy hoaxes.

For all this talk of guilt, I wonder whether anger is not a more appropriate emotion. For unease over how we live now is as much the result of a specific social and political context as it is an existential and irresolvable problem. On the publicity trail, I found that many were angered when they learned of the difference between what we are offered as compared with Northern Europe. If you struggle through one year of unpaid leave only to confront the "choice" of returning to full-time work using the babies' room at a crèche with one care-giver to five babies, or of leaving work altogether, then privatised guilt – blaming oneself – is not the most useful response. Nor is it simply a private grief if you wind up childless because most careers are carelessly predicated on the male life-pattern, circa 1950, of uninterrupted work. As Dowse says, the personal is political.

We can go round in circles on the question of how meaningful work is. Lam has discovered women who find work meaningful when her assumptions would have suggested otherwise. I have no doubt of it. The point of my jillaroo story is not to cast doubt on the value of work for everyone. It is not directly juxtaposed, as Dowse suggests, with the perils of a corporate life, but with my own love of my current work, and the exceptionally high morale among the publishers I work with. It precedes a consideration of the dilemmas of high-achieving women, where my working assumption is, clearly, that they have trained for and gained access to fulfilling jobs they will want – and have every right – to keep.

None of this changes the fact that some jobs are crappy, and that some of those doing them find caring for children, especially when they are small, preferable. I present evidence. The Scandinavian choice between a home-care allowance and job-protected leave, versus work and a child-care place, comes the closest I have seen to a genuinely "free choice" scenario. The home-care allowances have been hugely popular, and the take-up is highest among those in lower paid and lower status jobs. That said, work-centredness, as Hakim's data shows, can and does occur in every socio-economic group, including in the working class. Being child-centred can occur among the highly educated. But work-centredness of the type dominating our discussions is statistically *more* common among the upper echelons of workers. Women who go back to work early are more likely to be highly educated and affluent.

Lam raises the important issue of maternal depression, saying she would like to hear more on this. Again, space was limited. In the more comprehensive *Motherhood*, however, I deal with it in chapter five, while the entirety of chapter eight, beginning with the convicted child-killer Kathleen Folbigg, a middle-class stay-at-home mother, is devoted to the subject of mothering gone wrong. Because I follow the principle of the best interest of the child – rather than "motherhood as a religion," as Edgar alleges – I have no difficulty in acknowledging the importance of maternal depression or the occurrence of child abuse by mothers.

That said, on the topic of maternal depression we need precision rather than ideology. Maternal depression turns out to be a whole lot more complicated than what Jessie Bernard once famously claimed: that being a married housewife with children made you sick.

The Australian sociologist David De Vaus looked at this issue in 2002 for the Australian Institute of Family Studies. He showed that almost none of Bernard's propositions stand up in the light of contemporary data. De Vaus examined the 1997 National Survey of Mental Health and Wellbeing of Adults, the largest study of mental health ever conducted in Australia. As De Vaus pointed out, it offered a superb opportunity to test the Bernard thesis.

The key protection against depression was not work but long-term attachments, especially marriage. Married men and women were the *least likely* of any group to suffer mental-health problems (around 13 per cent). Married women with children were actually *much less at risk* of emotional disorders than any unmarried group, including working and non-working lone mothers, and single, childless working women. Being single, rather than being married, or working or not working, was the strongest risk factor for mental-health problems for *both* sexes. Twice as many divorced women, or 22.3 per cent, suffered from an anxiety disorder, as compared with 11 per cent of married women. Single, childless working women had almost double the rate of disorders as did married working mothers. De Vaus concluded: "Workforce participation and the absence of children and marriage is associated with considerably greater risk of mood, anxiety, and substance use disorders among women."

The US National Institute of Child Health and Human Development study on child-care data showed that child-care did not necessarily compensate for the effect of maternal depression on children. (This surprised me.) Parental influences were stronger than child-care, for good or ill. Moreover, children who went from poor parental care to a poor quality child-care centre did worst of all. If parental-care advocates should, indeed, think about maternal depression, it would be nice if just occasionally one also came across a child-care advocate who admitted that it is not the case that children automatically go from inadequate parents to top-notch child-care centres like the Perry Pre-school. Finally, George Brown and his colleagues' careful British studies showed that depression was least likely if women were able to fulfil their preferences – to work or not. Thus, policy should help them to achieve their desired role.

Dowse argues there is no risk-free policy. Quite so. Unhappily, however, she then goes on to mention Meredith Edwards. Edwards is lauded in *Sisters in Suits* as one who held the line against taxation assistance for stay-at-home mothers early in the Hawke-Keating era. Funds were allocated *on behalf of other women* on the presumption of where their interest lay: in the workforce.

This policy did not drive women of young children into the workforce in anything like the numbers that were hoped. Women continued to answer the imperatives of care. What happened instead was that the income of the vast majority of single-income families simply declined. The 1996 census data show that 55 per cent of women between the ages of 25 and 29 with a child under fifteen were not employed. Ann Harding's research shows that they joined the group of Australian families whose income put them just above the poverty line. No cost-free policy indeed.

That said, Edwards and others raised a very important issue about how family resources are distributed and, by implication, about a woman's need for economic independence. None of the policies I am advocating here sever a woman's connection to the labour market. They preserve it. It is not proposed that home-care allowances be provided in perpetuity, but during job-protected leave. Just as the ACTU did with its successful test case to the now defunct Industrial Relations Commission, I am taking parents' *actual* behaviour and looking for ways that we can surround it with new labour-market protections, to make the transition into caring roles and back to work both more seamless and safer.

There is another reason why we need to pay attention to women's economic capabilities. When women have greater economic power, they use it for children's advantage. Thus we should pay attention to those societies where women's economic productivity is arraigned not against the ethic of care, but on behalf of it.

In *Love & Money*, I expressed the hope that the new Labor government will not commit the mistakes of the early Blair government in embracing the neo-liberal Get to Work program and promoting early return to work and universal child-care. Later in Blair's term, the growing negative evidence on child-care prompted a significant shift, with two years of parental leave being granted, one year being paid, and the right given to request flexible work schedules.

So where do we presently stand? Rudd went to the 2020 Summit with his "big idea": universal parent and child centres. This was reported in the press as universal child-care centres for children from zero to five. In fact, as the full text of his speech to the Sydney Institute shows, his proposal was more nuanced. It was closer to *Love & Money*'s proposal of universal child and parent support centres. Such centres offer, in one local and readily identifiable place, a range of support services, such as maternal and baby health nurses, toy libraries, mothers' groups, playgroups, outreach services and so on. Such centres would be inclusive – directed at parents both in and out of the workforce. They would include child-care, but would not be restricted to it. In being small and local, they promise to recreate some of what the early feminists were hoping for in terms of parental involvement in community child-care centres.

Rudd's proposal, unfortunately, was couched in the market language of "one-stop shops," as Stephens notes. The suggestion that we allow for-profit operators to run the centres is worrying. Imagine an ABC Learning centre in every neighbourhood, mass-producing every aspect of early childhood! Parents might get a visit from the friendly ABC nurse shortly after the birth of their baby, who might insist that the ABC centre "gives children the best start in life," along with ABC formula milk. So baby is dropped off at child-care at 7 a.m., where they get the jab of immunisation provided by the pharmaceutical company which has cut a deal with ABC, to be collected at 7 p.m. along with a Big Mac and fries to go, because McDonald's has done likewise.

The missing element in Rudd's proposal is parental leave, an issue that is now before the Productivity Commission. Steve Biddulph says it is not the right body to consider this matter. He is right. One can recite in advance all the submissions along the lines of "For every $1 dollar invested, $7 will be returned." How is an economist to know that the beautiful set of numbers is false? May I, in the spirit of Swift, make a modest proposal? Let us have a Royal Commission into child-care and parental leave. Then, before a brilliant and remorseless QC, a Julian Burnside or Terry Tobin, let the child-care lobbyists be summoned as "expert" witnesses and be grilled, at risk of prosecution for perjury, to justify their claims.

The missing element in Rudd's early-childhood proposal, parental leave, was, however, supplied at the 2020 Summit: "An important priority is improved access to paid parental leave for parents (of children of varying ages) and carers (of the disabled and the aged). Parents need time to spend with their children, especially the very young, and should not be forced to return to work too early for financial reasons." The evidence that Australians would support such policies is strong. A recent Newspoll found 76 per cent of Australians supported paid maternity leave. An overwhelming 93 per cent thought that, "The most important thing for a baby in its first year of life is to have the full-time care of at least one parent."

One final point. In *Love & Money* I pointed out that women now hold a decisive political bargaining chip: fear over falling fertility. That concern can go one of two ways. It can become part of a productivity calculus, where women are pressured to go back to work ever earlier by carrot and stick: means-testing or cutting the baby bonus and targeting benefits almost exclusively to working mothers using child-care. Or it can be a basis on which to build a program to improve the condition of *all* mothers and parenthood generally. That won't happen without organisation.

It is vitally important that we recognise the need for some kind of parents' and carers' movement, tough-minded and politically savvy, an alliance of all those in or outside the paid labour force who supply or are in need of care. A troublesome, stroppy, well-informed, impossible-to-ignore group. Its aim would be to get onto the political agenda a program of justice for caregivers and those they care for. It needs to become a group to whom the media go when issues are raised, and one that politicians cannot afford to ignore. At the moment we have the Australian Family Association, defending the Christian family and the traditional division of labour. Many young, secular parents don't identify with that program. Meanwhile, the billion-dollar child-care industry wins the propaganda war, aided and abetted by child-care academics who should know better. At present, the only people putting some kind of fight against the McDonaldisation of childhood are lone voices, child psychologists like Steve Biddulph and independent writers like me.

Dowse says at the end of her response that there is more that unites us than divides us. I agree. Yet she also calls the status of care "intractable." No, it isn't. Now is the only time you will hear me quoting the free-market ideologue Friedrich Hayek. He said, "Nothing is inevitable but thinking makes it so." He is right. Where would the second-wave feminists have got if they adopted such a defeatist attitude towards the status of women? At the moment, we reward selfish individualism. We penalise altruism. That is what we must change.

Anne Manne

Steve Biddulph has been a psychologist for thirty years, and his books are in four million homes across the world. He co-led the *SIEV-X* memorial project, which can now be visited on the shores of Lake Burley Griffin in Canberra. He was Australian Father of the Year in 2000 and lives in the Tamar Valley in Tasmania.

Natasha Cica is director of the Hobart-based consultancy Periwinkle Projects. She has written about Australian politics and culture for the *Age*, the *Australian Financial Review Magazine* and *Griffith Review* and is working on a book about the legacy of the wilderness photographer Olegas Truchanas.

Sushi Das is a senior writer with the *Age*, where she has worked for twelve years. She is the winner of two Melbourne Press Club awards, including for best columnist in 2006.

Sara Dowse was the inaugural head of the prime minister's women's affairs section in the Whitlam and Fraser governments and drafted the ALP women's policy for the 1983 federal election. She is the author of *West Block*, set in the prime minister's department, and four other novels.

Don Edgar was the foundation director of the Australian Institute of Family Studies from 1980 to 1993. He is a member of the Victorian Children's Council. His next book (co-authored with his wife, Dr Patricia Edgar) is *The New Child: In Search of Smarter Grown-Ups*.

Virginia Haussegger presents ABC TV news in Canberra and writes a weekly column for the *Canberra Times*. Her book *Wonder Woman: The Myth of 'Having It All'* was published in 2005.

May Lam's Ph.D. was about the romance of feminism. In recent years she has worked on welfare-to-work policy for the not-for-profit sector in Australia, and for the government and private sector in the UK.

Anne Manne is a regular contributor to the *Age* and the *Monthly*. Her book *Motherhood: How Should We Care for Our Children?* was short-listed for the 2006 Walkley nonfiction book prize. She has written widely on feminism, motherhood, child-care, family policy, fertility and related issues.

Julie Stephens teaches politics and sociology at Victoria University. She was a Harold White Fellow at the National Library of Australia in 2007.

Paul Toohey is chief northern correspondent for the *Australian*. Before that he was a senior writer at the *Bulletin*. His first book, *God's Little Acre*, was published in 1996, followed by *Rocky Goes West* in 1997. His most recent book is *The Killer Within* (2007). He has won the Graham Perkin Journalist of the Year award and a Walkley award for magazine feature writing. He lives in Darwin.

Subscribe to Quarterly Essay

POST OR FAX THIS FORM TO: Quarterly Essay, Reply Paid 79448, Melbourne VIC 3000
Freecall: 1800 077 514 **Fax:** 61 3 9654 2290 **Email:** subscribe@blackincbooks.com

....

SUBSCRIPTIONS Receive a discount and never miss an issue. Mailed direct to your door.

1 year subscription (4 issues): $49 a year within Australia incl. GST. Outside Australia $79.

2 year subscription (8 issues): $95 a year within Australia incl. GST. Outside Australia $155.

* All prices include postage and handling.

....

BACK ISSUES Postage and handling is included.

- [ ] **QE 1** ($10.95) Robert Manne *In Denial*
- [ ] **QE 2** ($10.95) John Birmingham *Appeasing Jakarta*
- [ ] **QE 4** ($10.95) Don Watson *Rabbit Syndrome*
- [ ] **QE 5** ($12.95) Mungo MacCallum *Girt by Sea*
- [ ] **QE 6** ($12.95) John Button *Beyond Belief*
- [ ] **QE 7** ($12.95) John Martinkus *Paradise Betrayed*
- [ ] **QE 8** ($12.95) Amanda Lohrey *Groundswell*
- [ ] **QE 10** ($13.95) Gideon Haigh *Bad Company*
- [ ] **QE 11** ($13.95) Germaine Greer *Whitefella Jump Up*
- [ ] **QE 12** ($13.95) David Malouf *Made in England*
- [ ] **QE 13** ($13.95) Robert Manne with David Corlett *Sending Them Home*
- [ ] **QE 14** ($14.95) Paul McGeough *Mission Impossible*
- [ ] **QE 15** ($14.95) Margaret Simons *Latham's World*
- [ ] **QE 16** ($14.95) Raimond Gaita *Breach of Trust*
- [ ] **QE 17** ($14.95) John Hirst *'Kangaroo Court'*
- [ ] **QE 18** ($14.95) Gail Bell *The Worried Well*
- [ ] **QE 19** ($15.95) Judith Brett *Relaxed and Comfortable*
- [ ] **QE 20** ($15.95) John Birmingham *A Time for War*
- [ ] **QE 21** ($15.95) Clive Hamilton *What's Left?*
- [ ] **QE 22** ($15.95) Amanda Lohrey *Voting for Jesus*
- [ ] **QE 23** ($15.95) Inga Clendinnen *The History Question*
- [ ] **QE 24** ($15.95) Robyn Davidson *No Fixed Address*
- [ ] **QE 25** ($15.95) Peter Hartcher *Bipolar Nation*
- [ ] **QE 26** ($15.95) David Marr *His Master's Voice*
- [ ] **QE 27** ($15.95) Ian Lowe *Reaction Time*
- [ ] **QE 28** ($15.95) Judith Brett *Exit Right*
- [ ] **QE 29** ($16.95) Anne Manne *Love & Money*

....

PAYMENT DETAILS I enclose a cheque/money order made out to Schwartz Media Pty Ltd.
Please debit my credit card (Mastercard, Visa or Bankcard accepted).

Card No. [ ][ ][ ][ ][ ][ ][ ][ ][ ][ ][ ][ ][ ][ ][ ][ ]

Expiry date   /   Amount $

Cardholder's name   Signature

Name

Address

Email

Subscribe online at www.quarterlyessay.com